INSIDE THE MIND OF XI JINPING

FRANÇOIS BOUGON

Inside the Mind of
Xi Jinping

HURST & COMPANY, LONDON

First published in French by Actes Sud as *Dans la tête de Xi Jinping* in 2017.
This updated English edition published in the United Kingdom in 2018 by
C. Hurst & Co. (Publishers) Ltd.,
41 Great Russell Street, London, WC1B 3PL
© François Bougon and Actes Sud, 2017
Updates to the English edition © C. Hurst & Co. (Publishers) Ltd.
All rights reserved.
Printed in the United Kingdom

Translation © Vanessa Lee, 2018

Distributed in the United States, Canada and Latin America by
Oxford University Press, 198 Madison Avenue, New York, NY 10016,
United States of America.

The right of François Bougon to be identified as the author
of this publication is asserted by him in accordance with the
Copyright, Designs and Patents Act, 1988.

A Cataloguing-in-Publication data record for this book
is available from the British Library.

ISBN: 9781849049849

This book is printed using paper from registered sustainable
and managed sources.

www.hurstpublishers.com

To Julie

CONTENTS

INTRODUCTION

THE 'CHINESE DREAM'

On 17 January 2017, a communist leader found himself applauded by the global capitalist elite assembled at the exclusive ski resort of Davos. As the first Chinese leader to take part in the World Economic Forum, Xi Jinping made an impact and won approval. Before politicians and businessmen rattled by Brexit in the United Kingdom, and in the presence of the populist US president-elect Donald Trump, Xi championed globalisation and offered to heal their emotional ills:

> As a line in an old Chinese poem goes, 'Honey melons hang on bitter vines; sweet dates grow on thistles and thorns.' In a philosophical sense, nothing is perfect in the world. One would fail to see the full picture if one claimed something to be perfect because of its merits, or if something were viewed as useless just because of its defects. It is true that economic globalization has created new problems, but this is no justification for writing off economic globalization completely.

Three days before Trump's investiture as president, Xi defended the Davos participants' perceived and cherished world order, and implicitly criticized the solutions put forward by Trump, be it the closure of borders or restrictions on free trade. 'We should commit ourselves to growing an open global economy to share opportunities and interests through opening-up, and achieve win-win outcomes. One should not just retreat to the harbour when encountering a storm, for this will never get us to the other side of the ocean,' he said, adding a reference to another Chinese saying: 'people with petty shrewdness attend to trivial matters, while people with vision attend to the governance of institutions'.

Quite a PR victory for the man who sees himself as the advocate not only of world trade and international cooperation, but also of the Paris climate agreements. But who is this man, nominated general secretary of the Party in 2012, then reappointed for a second term five years later at the Nineteenth Congress? Who is this leader who has consolidated his power to such a degree as to have his name inscribed in the Chinese Communist Party constitution, a privilege that only Mao Zedong, founder of the Party, has previously enjoyed in his lifetime?

Without question, it can be said that Xi Jinping (pronounced "sh-yee gin ping") is the 'product' of a system. It is a system that was born at the end of the 1920s amidst the guerrillas of China's south-eastern mountains, who would go on to defeat Chang Kai-shek's Nationalists after the Long March and the Civil War. The country traditionally divides its leaders into generations. The 'Great Helmsman' Mao Zedong, the revolutionary leader and founder of the People's Republic of China in 1949, belongs to the first of these generations. From 1943 to 1976, he championed a permanent revolution, putting class struggle at the heart of his policies, mobilising the country in relentless political campaigns, and leading it dangerously close to collapse and chaos during the Cultural Revolution. Deng Xiaoping, 'the Little Helmsman' (1978–89), presided over the second generation, to whom fell the task of fixing Mao's deadly follies by opening up the country to capitalism and laying the foundations of its economic renewal.

Deng placed Jiang Zemin at the head of the Party (1989–2002) following an internal crisis brought about by the Tiananmen democratic movement, which ended in bloody repression and the side-lining of proponents of more daring political reforms. The fourth generation was personified by a leader devoid of charisma, the engineer Hu Jintao (2002–12). In contrast to his predecessor, Xi Jinping, representing the fifth generation, stands out—there is undeniably more to him. He possessed precisely the right amount of charisma and panache required to move effortlessly up the Party's ranks, yet without coming across as a threat to potential rivals. This perfect match with the system and its era has been particularly remarkable.

All the more so since Xi is, after Deng, the Chinese leader who has accumulated the most power, first as leader of the Party from 2012 and then as president from 2013. In this position, he has established his authority by following the tried and tested tactic of his predecessors: making sure not to commit any blunders and pampering the 'elders'—grandees such as Jiang Zemin, now in his nineties. To gain control of the Party's immense bureaucratic machine and circumvent potential opposition, Xi swiftly set up several 'leading small groups' that reported directly to him. In November 2012, he established a commission responsible for Taiwanese and Foreign Affairs, then, a year a later, one overseeing economic reforms. In January 2014, a national security commission was created; a month later came a cybersecurity and computerisation commission, followed by another on national defence and military reform; and, in June that year, a commission for economic and financial affairs. This strategy of encirclement has proven effective. Step by step, these special commissions have enabled Xi to impose his ideas on the Party's traditional organs, such as its Standing Committee, where he has to deal with representatives of different factions, born of political disagreement or personal rivalries. All of which has led the Australian sinologist Geremie R. Barmé to dub him 'China's CEO' or 'Chairman of Everything'.

Xi Jinping is also a *hong er dai*, literally a 'Second-Generation Red', the son of a revolutionary pioneer. It is his turn to make history, and hereditary legitimacy is not without significance for a leader who intends to fight on the ideological front. He is now called upon to preside over the fate of the world's second largest economy, at the precise moment when the regime needs to find a new model for development. Mao promoted class struggle—'a revolution is not a dinner party'—and Deng and his successors, the market, coining the now celebrated oxymoron 'Socialist Market Economy'. At the Nineteenth Party Congress in November 2017, Xi announced the beginning of a 'New Era' for China as a great power, pursuing its path to becoming the world's largest economy and intent on reclaiming the 'centre stage'.

When he first took office, time was of the essence. The Party was concerned about its survival. How could we tell, one might ask, when it comes to a regime as impenetrable as the Vatican? By means of selected readings. Wang Qishan, who spearheads the fight against corruption within the Party, distributed far and wide copies of Alexis de Tocqueville's *The Old Regime and the Revolution*. Once published, the translation of this 1856 text was an overnight success. Yet what precisely is its argument? In essence, that the French monarchy was swept away by the Revolution even though the country was prosperous, and reforms underway to tackle corruption and inequality. It has all the trappings of a cautionary tale for today's China.

Was Xi one of those who read the text on Wang's recommendation? We cannot know. Power in China has increasingly sealed itself off as the country has asserted itself on the international stage. Jiang Zemin readily accepted interviews with foreign journalists; Hu did occasionally, but only collectively. Xi, on the other hand, never gives interviews to the Western media and his close advisors are equally inaccessible. He does write a great deal, however. Since he started out as a mere local cadre in the 1980s, he has never ceased to pen articles, books, and speeches.

In fact, on 1 October 2014, China's national day, a 500-page volume was published entitled *The Governance of China*, a compendium of speeches and other texts by Xi Jinping compiled by the State Council's—or Chinese government's—Information Office and the Party Central Committee's Central Policy Research Office. In these texts, Xi expressed his views on a number of topics, from domestic policy to diplomacy. Foreign editions were soon available. The cover—always the same in every country of publication—features an image of the president redolent of 1960s portraits of Mao at the height of his personality cult. Easily spotted, the book made headlines when official Chinese media published a photograph taken at Facebook's Californian headquarters, during a visit by China's then chief internet censor, Lu Wei: a copy of the English edition featured prominently in Mark Zuckerberg's office.

If Xi at first castigated the evasive and overblown style of Party rhetoric, it now appears that he has come perfectly to terms with it. His speeches do not show any attempt at elegance. He has complied with the practices of the Party and slipped into its heavy stylistic mire, reproducing even its most exasperating mannerisms. It represents a form of 'Newspeak', where everything claims to be new ('new normal') and necessarily dialectical ('double non-negation'), and where no reality is safe from being declined into several points—'four consciences', 'four tones' or 'four completelys', 'eight obligations', 'two studies and one behaviour'. And yet it is in these declarations that Xi Jinping's sources of inspiration and political leanings reside, or at least where they can be glimpsed.

Xi Jinping does not only write; he also reads a considerable amount. At least, that is what he claims. His travels abroad serve as an opportunity for him to show off his literary knowledge. In 2015, during a visit to the United States, he claimed to have read the revolutionary Thomas Paine's *Common Sense*, as well as the works of Henry David Thoreau, Walt Whitman, Mark Twain and Ernest Hemingway:

> I was most captivated by *The Old Man and the Sea* and its descriptions of the howling wind, the pouring rain, the roaring waves, the little boat, the old man, and the sharks. So when I visited Cuba for the first time, I went specially to the Cojimar dam where Hemingway wrote the book. On my second visit, I went to the bar Hemingway frequented and ordered a mojito, his favourite rum with mint leaves and ice. I wanted to feel

for myself what had been on his mind and the very place he was when he wrote those stories. I believe it is always important to make the effort to gain a deeper understanding of the cultures and civilizations that differ from our own.

In Russia, during the 2014 Sochi Winter Olympics, he gave a list—and a long one at that—of his favourite Russian authors: Krylova, Pushkin, Gogol, Lermontov, Turgenev, Dostoyevsky, Nekrasov, Chernyshevsky, Tolstoy and Chekhov. A month earlier, he had done the same in France: Montesquieu, Voltaire, Rousseau, Diderot, Saint-Simon, Fourier, Sartre, Montaigne, La Fontaine, Molière, Stendhal, Balzac, Hugo, Dumas *père* and *fils*, George Sand, Flaubert, Maupassant, Romain Rolland and Jules Verne. In Germany, too, he was sure to enumerate his reading habits: Goethe, Schiller, Heine, Leibniz, Kant, Hegel, Feuerbach, Heidegger, and Marcuse. Too bad for Mexico, where the Chinese leader only cited Octavio Paz.

In October 2014, in a speech on arts and literature aimed at a local Chinese audience, Xi beat his own record in referring to 114 Chinese and foreign writers, painters, calligraphers, philosophers, musicians, dancers, choreographers, sculptors, and dramatists. Whether in coquetry or vanity, his erudition apparently reached as far back as the *The Epic of Gilgamesh*, the mythical narrative from Mesopotamia, and the Vedas, the sacred texts of Ancient India.

INTRODUCTION

When I asked the dissident writer Murong Xuecun about his president's passion for reading, he replied ironically: 'My friends came up with a list of all the books he claims to have read. It is impressive. He is doubtless the most well-read Chinese leader since the birth of China. But really, does he have time to read? I don't believe so. In China, it has even become a joke. One of my friends told me that straight after his Russian visit, where he claimed to love reading Dostoyevsky, Xi had also cited two Chinese writers who owe their fame to the internet. One is a nationalist author, Zhou Xiaoping. "How can someone who loves reading Dostoyevsky like Zhou Xiaoping?" my friend asked me. It makes no sense. So I don't believe that Xi Jinping has read all of books he says he has.' A videographer once made a parody montage of all these 'literary' speeches. Like most satire against the president, it was quickly censored in China.

But whether or not he is a gifted literary scholar, Xi Jingping faces a considerable challenge: to keep in power the party for which his father fought as a guerrilla in the northwest; and to find a new economic model more respectful of people's health and the environment, after thirty years of growth based on cheap labour and exports. Xi Jinping and the other 'red princes', descendants of the first revolutionaries now at the helm of the country, have been called upon to save their fathers' legacy. If all goes well, Xi will preside at the Chinese Communist Party's grandiose centenary celebrations in 2021.

How does he do it? How does Xi perceive his role? What are his beliefs, his convictions, as China, officially Marxist, has become an ultra-capitalist and profoundly unequal country threatened by corruption? This is what I shall attempt to answer throughout this book, drawing on interviews with Chinese and Western intellectuals, but even more so on readings of Xi's theoretical texts, which remain the best indicator of his intellectual education and influences; significantly, some of the more nationalist and aggressively anti-Western texts have not been translated into English by the state propaganda services.

Though he portrayed himself at the 2017 Davos summit as the international protector of free trade, against a protectionist Donald Trump, Xi is instituting a form of neo-authoritarianism at home, bolstered by a strong state. Xi is taking advantage of the economic and ideological weaknesses of Western democracies to carry forward China as the second-largest world power, treading a path between references to 1940s and '50s Maoism and harnessing a thousand-year traditional culture. He forges ahead in the name of the 'Chinese dream'—a reference borrowed from the rival United States, which China could supplant as the world's greatest economic power by 2030. But of what does this dream consist? To better understand this new Chinese way, one must follow in the footsteps of Pascal: 'China makes things obscure, you say. And I reply: China makes things obscure, but there is light to be found. Seek it out.'

1

THE RENAISSANCE MAN

On 15 November 2012, the world was waiting, and the Chinese top brass were playing hard to get. Such was the prerogative of the new leaders of an almighty power now fit to rival the United States, the same China that had showed its strength four years earlier during the Beijing Olympics. A degree of impatience, tinged with excitement, filled the crowd of hand-picked journalists who had rushed to the Great Hall of the People, a massive 1950s building boasting kitsch Stalinist décor. As in the good old days of the Soviet Union, reporters shared competing interpretations of this surprising delay. Almost an hour! Didn't it seem that Xi Jinping had disappeared from the political scene just before his investiture, fuelling the maddest of rumours? At the back of the room, cameramen and photographers were growing impatient. Outside, the Beijing winter sun was shining—the Chinese Communist Party (CCP), master of the elements, can always make the pollution disappear for important occasions, even if it involves closing down factories.

The seven members of the Standing Committee of the Politburo, the heart of power in China, were finally about to make their appearance, to the relief of the audience, whose whispers immediately ceased. Treading the red carpet, they approached one by one in their order of precedence, in a well-rehearsed *mise en scène*. The master of ceremonies declared: 'May I ask you to join me in giving them a warm welcome!' A fraction of the journalists applauded.

Smiling, the Standing Committee waved at the crowd. In the background, in the classical style of traditionalist painters, was a huge painting of a mountain. The Great Wall was also there. 'Sorry to have kept you waiting,' said Xi Jinping, before introducing the Committee's other members—Li Keqiang, Zhang Dejiang, Yu Zhengsheng, Liu Yunshan, Wang Qishan and Zhang Gaoli—and delivering a twenty-minute speech. This 'meeting with the press' did not allow any time for questions. It was a merely an occasion to parade the new heads of China and their leader, Xi Jinping. In their world, the media are not there to question, but to celebrate.

The images presented were calibrated for official Chinese television and the foreign media, broadcasting the investiture ceremony live. These seven men—gender equality is not yet on the Chinese government's agenda—all between 59 and 66 years of age, adhered to an identical dress code: tie, white shirt, black suit, well-polished shoes, and not a strand of white hair despite their age. Dyeing one's hair jet black is compulsory; in China it is a sign of a powerful man, and a powerful man cannot allow time to leave its mark. The next day, a single photograph—mocked by the online community as redolent of the film *Reservoir Dogs*, minus the sunglasses—made the front page of every Chinese newspaper, by order of the Party: the propaganda machine's show of power.

Only the 'number six' in the hierarchy—Wang Qishan, head of anti-corruption—had indulged in a bit of colour: he was wearing a blue tie. The other ties were red, the colour of the revolution, over which 'Pekinologists' were about to have a field day. But the most eagerly expected of these 'seven samurais' was of course the new Party chairman: the 'new emperor', Xi Jinping, who had been tentatively singled out five years previously as next in line to govern the world's most populous country, with over 1.3 billion inhabitants.

Xi differed from his predecessor, Hu Jintao. The latter embodied to the point of caricature the grey and dreary bureaucrat, tasteless and lacklustre, the apparatchik master of stonewalling and soporific speeches. While the two characters that make up his given name, Jinping, signify 'close to peace', Xi Jinping possessed a strong personality, and undeniable powers of seduction.

'He radiates incredible strength,' claims a European diplomat posted in the Chinese capital. Everyone who's been near him says that Xi demonstrates the tranquil assurance of the 'heirs'—of members of the 'red caste', the communist élite. He has no need to raise his voice, and in meetings he exudes a natural charisma. 'Hu Jintao was fundamentally an administrator, an employee, he spoke with the embarrassment of those who feel out of place. Xi is the heir of [a revolutionary] family, he speaks as though he were at home,' explains the Chinese historian Zhang Lifan.

Xi Jinping (b. 1953) belongs to the generation of 'educated youth' who were born in the 1950s and sent to the countryside during the Cultural Revolution (1966–76). There they were re-educated amongst the peasants, for some after a spell as fanatic Red Guards, Mao's 'little generals'. This Chinese-style 1968 generation, coddled in their youth by the conquests and progress of the young communist regime, discovered a completely different reality in rural China. To escape it, this generation had to negotiate between cynicism and ambition. A former Red Guard turned businessman and poet, Huang Nubo, aptly summarises their state of mind: 'The Cultural Revolution taught my generation that you had to act like a wolf to survive ... The winner takes it all. If you beat someone, you are a hero, and if you are rich, you are right.'

Xi Jinping, who grew up in the Beijing neighbourhoods inhabited by senior officials, did not seek wealth.

It was power that attracted him. According to the statements of a former acquaintance, gathered by the American Embassy between 2007 and 2009, Xi was always 'particularly ambitious' and 'never lost track of his goal', which was to reach the highest echelons. 'Xi is not corrupt nor is he interested in money, but you could say he has been "corrupted by power"', claims the same diplomatic telegram, dated 16 November 2009.

When Singapore's prime minister, Lee Kuan Yew, advocate of 'Asian values', met Xi Jinping in 2007, just after the latter's election to the Politburo, Xi made a strong impression:

> He has his own mind, he has experienced much, and gone through many a difficult period. He spent seven years in the countryside, then eighteen years in Fujian and Zhejiang provinces, before going to Shanghai. I would put him in Nelson Mandela's class of people. A person with enormous emotional stability who does not allow his personal misfortunes or sufferings to affect his judgment.

Xi Jinping is above all a *zuofeng*, a 'style', as the Chinese say. This was much discussed during the first months of his term. Xi not only had charisma, but he adopted a relaxed way of expressing himself, shedding his predecessor's cold and bureaucratic manner. The private and professional behaviour of officials are at the heart of his discourse: he has called for more simplicity, and less luxury and overindulgence.

In this quest for an exemplary Communist Party official, he evoked the 'golden age' of Maoism, the 1940s and 1950s. This was the Communists' time of conquest, appearing as a model to rival that of the discredited Guomindang (National Party). Founded in 1921, the Party came to power in 1949 with the promise of a new China, fairer and less corrupt; a China that would contrast with the pomp and eccentricities of Chiang Kaishek's Republic of China. Yet, since the last years of Hu's presidency, a string of scandals has unveiled the excesses of local dignitaries unscrupulously enriching themselves, surrounding themselves with mistresses, and practising nepotism.

For Xi, this has degraded the image of the Party, and threatened it. Just before becoming president, several cases tarnished the final months of Hu Jintao's mandate. First, the revelations provoked by the fall of Bo Xilai, one of the regime's 'cherished sons', another 'prince's son' and one of Xi's greatest rivals—his father, Bo Yibo, was one of Mao's comrades-in-arms. He was accused of abuse of power, corruption, and having covered up his wife's murder of a British citizen. Then came the revelations in the Western media of the personal fortunes of former prime minister Wen Jiabao's relations. Henceforth, under Xi's rule, not a day would pass without the media reporting on the fall of an official in the fight against corruption. This involved tracking the 'flies' (*cangying*) and tigers (*laohu*), the low- and high-ranking officials—

another concept borrowed from the 1950s—but also the 'big tigers' (*dahu*), dignitaries who have fled abroad following the embezzlement of public funds, and who are wanted by the authorities. This would be a large-scale purge, affecting hundreds of thousands of officials.

Xi, the modern-looking heir, has been unwavering in his ambition: his mission is to save the Party inherited from his father and his peers, by returning it to its former ideological legitimacy, through a mixture of Chinese philosophy, Maoism and nationalism, and by fighting against 'deviant behaviour'.

During a meeting of China's anti-corruption unit, the Central Commission for Discipline Inspection, on 22 January 2013, Xi Jinping asserted his determination to 'clean up' the Party. 'Work practices are not a futile issue,' he underlined. 'If we do not decisively correct unhealthy practices, and if we allow them to continue, then they will become an invisible wall shutting off the Party from the masses, the Party will therefore lose its foundations, its veins and its strength.' During this same meeting, Xi explained that he wished 'to bring power into the cage of the institution', a colourful way of showing his desire to institute 'counter-powers' against the abuses and excesses of officials. He insisted that 'no Party member may impose their own private interest and claim privileges'.

It would appear that the moral correction of the Party had been a long-standing plan of Xi Jinping's. He foregrounded the issue in his first speech to the media as general secretary of the Party, on 15 November 2012:

> Our party is a political party that serves the people wholeheartedly. The party has led the people in scoring accomplishments that capture the attention of the world. We have every reason to be proud. However, we are proud but not complacent, and we will never rest on our laurels. In the new situation, our party faces many severe challenges, and there are many pressing problems within the party that need to be resolved, especially problems such as corruption and bribe-taking by some party members and cadres, being out of touch with the people, placing undue emphasis on formality and bureaucracy, must be addressed with great effort. The whole party must be vigilant. The metal itself must be hard to be turned into iron.

Much like the metaphor employed—wrought iron, evoking the image of a slicing sword—this first speech was hard-hitting. At the same time, a subtle balance of essence and form was detectable in the use of everyday words to impress, if not tacitly to threaten. The delivery was fluid. Xi seemed almost relaxed.

A completely cool Chinese leader? The then US vice-president had a different impression. He saw in Xi the throes of responsibility: 'He is a strong, bright man, but he has the look of a man who is not at all sure all is going to end well,' Joe Biden would tell University of Pennsylvania students in May 2013, following a ten-day trip to China.

From the US itself, Xi has borrowed, somewhat mockingly, a mythical formula: the American Dream has become the 'Chinese Dream' (*Zhongguo meng*), a hold-all concept that allows him to glorify recovered greatness and flatter nationalist sensitivities. Washington is the great rival against which China must always compete. This was noted in 1988 during a study trip by Wang Huning, an academic from Shanghai who in 1995 became one of the government's foremost theorists under General Secretary Jiang Zemin, before joining the inner sanctum of Xi Jinping's Politburo Standing Committee in November 2017. Wang published a book based on his American experience. *America against America* outlines his six months spent in the US, where he attempted to develop his understanding of the world's largest economy, of its strengths and its weaknesses. The responsibility of the Chinese intellectual, he wrote at the time, was to understand why China, a 2,000-year-old civilisation, went into decline, while the United States, a young country of only 200 years' history, became the world's number one economic power. 'I believe that it is the duty of an intellectual living in the twentieth century to study these two phenomena. Every Chinese intellectual must do so; it is the best way to understand the world and oneself and to explore China's path towards power and prosperity.' Prosperity and its opposite, decline, are issues that continually haunt the Party.

Today, Xi Jinping believes that in 2021, the hundredth anniversary of the founding of the Party, China will have overtaken its rival thanks to the emergence of a 'well-to-do' society (*xiaokang shehui*), a concept taken from Confucianism. In 2049, the hundredth anniversary of the People's Republic of China, Xi predicts a 'modern, prosperous, powerful, democratic, civilised and harmonious socialist country'. And, it goes without saying, a leading world power. These are the 'two objectives for the centenary' highlighted in the majority of his speeches. He referred to them during his lengthy speech—almost 3.5 hours in duration—on 18 October 2017, during the opening of the nineteenth Party Congress, halfway through his presidential mandate. Now, he argued with due Marxist diligence that, to concretise these objectives, the Party needs to resolve the main contradiction facing contemporary Chinese society: 'between unbalanced and inadequate development and the people's ever-growing needs for a better life.'

Xi first talked in public about this 'Chinese Dream' fifteen days after his investiture as Party chairman, on 29 November 2012. The context of this speech was no coincidence. Along with other members of the Standing Committee, he chose to visit the new National Museum of China—no tie this time, just a shirt and jacket. The building is located opposite the Great Hall of the People, on the eastern side of Tiananmen Square. No expense was spared by the regime for its construction: the renovation cost about £221 million and the building has a total floor space of about 192,000 square metres. The only larger museum in the world is the Louvre, home of the famous *Mona Lisa* so favoured by Chinese tourists, which covers 210,000 square metres. Xi visited the permanent exhibition 'The Road to Rejuvenation' (*fuxing-zhilu*). Translations of *fuxing* vary; it can mean 'renaissance', 'rejuvenation', or 'recovery'. Yet, whatever the r-word, the epoch in question is the return of a strong and powerful China to the world stage, a place it had given up to the West in the nineteenth century. *Fuxing* is meant to suggest a new vigour, a regained pride. Covering a period from the treaties imposed by Western colonial powers in the nineteenth century to the economic dynamism of the end of the twentieth century, the exhibition is an account of the regime's current historiography, and an outline of the ideological underpinnings of the 'Chinese Dream'.

In the first surprise of the exhibition, the communist leaders designate themselves the heirs to 5,000 years of history, to the great imperial China, feudalism, the invention of gunpowder and the compass. The rupture of the 1949 socialist revolution is not mentioned. They are also presented as the makers of the country's new impetus and consequently as its avengers. In this vein, recent history cannot be understood without an awareness of the affronts represented by the arrival of Westerners and imposition of the 'unequal treaties' throughout the nineteenth century. This discourse of humiliation was in fact constructed by the Nationalists at the end of the 1920s following the death of Sun Yat-sen. Up until that point, the first Opium War had been deemed a 'quarrelsome side-story', a 'dispute', an 'expedition', but not 'the aggrieved, unprecedented national tragedy' it has become. The trace of this humiliation is still palpable today in the Chinese president's speeches on symbolic dates. The 'sick man of Asia' must be erased.

Thus, on 1 October 2009, for the sixtieth anniversary of the People's Republic of China, Hu Jintao, in a Mao-style outfit, exclaimed: 'Today, socialist China is standing firm in the East, facing the future.' And in his first speech as president, Xi Jinping would declare, 'Every Chinese citizen who lives in this great country at this great time has the chance to succeed in life, to see their dream become reality, to progress and fulfil themselves at the same time as their homeland and their time.' The expression 'at this great time' is of significance: now is the time when China will recover its greatness.

The museum circuit through the permanent exhibition promotes the idea of this recovered power. Unsurprisingly, the most controversial episodes of Chinese communist history—such as the abuses and millions of victims of Maoism (the Great Leap Forward and the Cultural Revolution), and the repression of the June 1989 democratic movement following weeks of nationwide demonstrations—are glossed over or played down. He who controls the past controls the future.

The second surprise of the exhibition is the way in which it draws upon a form of nationalism that embraces not only the inevitable figure of Mao Zedong, the country's liberator and founder of the 'New China', but also a figure whom Mao despised, Confucius. Confucian thought, developed by hundreds of disciples after his death in 479 BCE, fed into the political philosophy of the emperors. Plato's equal within the pantheon of classical philosophers, Confucius fits perfectly into this new communist historiography, obsessed with the idea of power and of a 'great country'. A civilisation worthy of the name needs several 'great men', a preferably millennial tradition, and cultural influence. Even if this goes against the prejudices of older communist leaders.

At the end of his visit, the new party leader Xi made a speech without referring to notes, placing the start of his mandate under the banner of the 'Chinese Dream'. The expression was picked up by the state propaganda machine and plastered across the walls of every city. 'After more than one hundred and seventy years of struggle since the Opium War, the great renewal of the Chinese nation can finally glimpse a bright future,' he asserted. 'Today, the whole world speaks of the "Chinese Dream". In my view, to realise the great renewal of the nation is the greatest dream of the Chinese people since the start of the modern era,' he added.

One of the routes towards this cultural renewal is the promotion of traditions. As he would later explain on 19 August 2013, during the 'National Conference on Ideological Work and Communication', 'traditional

Chinese culture and its mighty cultural soft power are two of the nation's most notable advantages'. Here Xi developed a line of thought in fact originating in the early 2000s. China, then in the midst of its economic boom and starting to make itself known on the world stage, was going through an identity crisis. What were the essential characteristics of a 'great nation' (*daguo*)? The Hu government launched a series of studies into the question.

On 24 November 2003, leaders organised a Politburo study session. This is a regular practice for the Chinese elite, who often come together to debate an issue. Experts are invited to give their opinion, then the general secretary gives a speech, which sets the tone. On this occasion, the study day focused on 'the history of the development of the greatest nations since the fifteenth century'. The fifteenth century was the pivotal moment when Western history sped up, while China stayed put. Once more the fear of decline was rearing its head. Two historians were invited, Qi Shirong and Qian Chengdan. The first, who died in 2015 at the age of 89, was a pioneer in Chinese global history; the second is an expert on Britain. For more than two hours, they presented the fate of nine countries that successively ruled the world before falling into a phase of decline: Portugal, Spain, the Netherlands, the United Kingdom, France, Germany, Japan, Russia (the Soviet Union), and the United States.

Qian Chengdan gave his account of this slightly odd seminar soon after its conclusion: 'The participants were not your average students, and these were not classes either. The choice of subject was, in itself, a very interesting and visionary decision. China was in the middle of the globalisation process. As academics, we asserted and underlined very early on that Chinese modernisation had to observe what had taken place in other countries. At the end of the day we are modernising ourselves after the others: many have preceded us in the process. Some have had a lot of success, but there are a few lessons to be learned from their failures. The lessons to be learned from the failures are perhaps even more numerous than those to be learned from the successes.'

In his speech at the end of this session, President Hu, in the spirit of Marxism, reminded the audience of the importance of dialectical materialism, and historical materialism. He added that, contrary to the predictions of American thinker Francis Fukuyama in *The End of History and the Last Man*, history had not ended after the fall of the Soviet bloc. China had not only held fast, but was also ready to take on a more important role—and it could not afford to miss out on the opportunity. 'As history has always shown, opportunities are extremely precious, but they are also fleeting,' he warned. 'In the current circumstances, we must focus even more on the study of historical knowledge and of Chinese history, especially that of the Revolution, to educate officials and the people. We must not only study Chinese history, but world history as well, for we need an in-depth vision of national and world histories.' Records of the meeting were subsequently distributed throughout the Party ranks, and officials were ordered to study the material carefully.

In China, no one has forgotten this study session, for it led to the broadcast of a great documentary epic in November 2006 on state television's economics channel, CCTV-2. Entitled 'The Rise of the Great Powers', the series consisted of twelve 1-hour episodes.

'One morning at the end of November 2013, as I was going to work, I heard a news item on the radio,' the director, Ren Xue'an, explained at the time. 'The Central Politburo was going to embark on a collective study of the history of the development of nine great powers since the fifteenth century. In the stifling hubbub of Beijing's third ring-road, I suddenly heard the call of a vast and buried history and the idea continued to excite me.' He was assisted by Qian Chengdan, the historian who had taken part in the Politburo study session.

The enterprise took three years. Seven film crews were sent across the globe. The investment was commensurate to the challenge. State television made its resources available to the historians. The result is fascinating, a far cry from traditional propaganda. Even Western viewers could let themselves be carried along by the fate of these great powers, from fifteenth-century Portugal to today's United States.

The final part of the documentary, entitled 'Thoughts on the Great Path', made the government's intentions very clear. Even though China is never mentioned in this episode, the whole world is made aware that it will in turn one day become a great power. But how to avoid the decline experienced by other countries? There is no clear-cut solution: it is important to master technological innovation, to make use of hard as well as soft power, to be a united nation, to have a flourishing economy and a stable political system. The danger, the historians point out, lies in the temptation of imperialism and hegemonic aspirations—a veiled criticism of the United States, termed a 'superpower' in the documentary. If there is a subliminal message to be taken from the series, it is in the final episode's excerpt of an interview with former French president Valéry Giscard d'Estaing, a great friend of the Chinese government: 'The rise of a civilised power such as China with its great cultural and intellectual tradition that goes back to its early days, is a benefit for the planet'.

The series, accompanied by the release of eight books, was a real success. However, there was some criticism from both sides of the political spectrum, from both hard-line Maoist purists and the liberals (China specialists term as 'liberals' the advocates of public freedoms and defenders of civil society). The former believed too much focus was given to the market economy. The latter saw the series as praising authoritarianism. Amongst these liberal voices, the writer and essayist Liu Xiaobo, future political prisoner and Nobel Prize laureate, expressed his concern:

Before the rapid emergence of the economic power of this great dictatorial country, if its rise encounters no obstacles, if we continue to call for [internal] calm, we run the risk of seeing history repeat itself, and the results will not only be catastrophic for the Chinese people but also for the development of freedom and democracy on a global scale. Hence, to contain the negative effects of the rise of a dictatorship on global civilisation, free countries need to help the biggest dictatorship in the world to transform itself into a free and democratic state.

At the time of writing in 2018, no one intends to get in the way of China's development. This great reflection on the nature of power in the 2000s provided the intellectual fodder for the conception of the Beijing Olympics, which opened in August 2008. Xi Jinping, vice-president at the time, was its grand commissar, entrusted with the final preparations. For the opening ceremony, he hired the filmmaker Zhang Yimou, who had become a sort of official director of the regime's great spectacles. Performed in front of an audience of 90,000, including eighty foreign heads of state, the opening ceremony was grandiose, impressive, martial: 2,008 *fou*, traditional drums, were beaten in time by 2,008 extras. It was a historical moment; the Olympic Games had been a 'hundred-year-old dream', according to the official propaganda, and presented the perfect opportunity to unfold the new 'national story' before the entire world, the '5,000 years of history' asserted by the Party, in all its splendour—and not in its horror, the dreadfulness of the Mao era.

Xi was already, at the time of the Games, convinced that this was how Chinese history had to be rewritten. Confucius and Mao Zedong were the guests of honour. A quotation from the *Analects* opened the festivities: 'What a joy to welcome friends from afar!' The official programme went even further, explaining the phrase: 'The Chinese people warmly welcome their friends who have come from around the world, according to a practice inherited from ancient Chinese civilisation'. It is important to point out here that in April 2007 a hundred academics, university researchers and professors had signed a petition, featured on two dozen websites, demanding that the Chinese Olympic delegation wear traditional Chinese clothing for the opening ceremony. This was to no avail, but the movement spread. One of the two biggest Beijing universities, Beida, launched a competition for ideas to replace the Western toga, worn during the medal ceremony, with a Chinese-inspired outfit. 'Why should Chinese students wear Western togas?' asked Sui Yue, president of the student society that had co-organised the competition with the Young Communist League. In 2007, students of Tsinghua, one of the most prestigious universities in the country, were to be found strutting around campus dressed in outfits inspired by Han dynasty (206 BCE–220 CE) costumes, distinguishable by their large sleeves, large tunics, and lack of buttons. The students were showing off their newfound Chinese pride.

Significantly, Xi has promoted one other historical figure: Zheng He, the navigator who, during the Ming Dynasty, went on seven naval expeditions (1405–33) and reached the coast of Africa. In other words, this was yet another reference to the turning point that came in the fifteenth century, to which Chinese historiography obstinately returns: the era of the conquering empire, before China turned in on itself and left the field open to Western powers. The memory of this explorer has been a means for China to articulate its new maritime ambitions. After taking office, Xi Jinping would refer to Zheng again, in order to promote a more specific project, 'the new maritime silk road'. Before the Indonesian Parliament on 3 October 2013, Xi reminded his audience that the admiral had stopped over in the archipelago on one of his voyages. 'These visits left a trail of lovely stories of friendly exchanges between the Chinese and the Indonesians that are still told today,' he pointed out, even if this significantly idealises the matter.

Xi's China embraces a grandiose past, and projects itself into an even more splendid future. As for the man himself, he will be the orchestrator of this success; he will fulfil unfulfilled promises. His future lies in China's past.

2

THE 'ANTI-GORBACHEV'

It was March 2016, and I was in Beijing. Among the new books on display in a fashionable bookshop, one volume in particular caught my eye: the Chinese edition of *Secondhand Time: The Last of the Soviets*. My first reaction was one of surprise. How could this book be given the honour of a translation into Chinese? The Belarusian Svetlana Alexievich had just been awarded the Nobel Prize for Literature a month previously, for her writings critical of Soviet power—'a monument to suffering and courage', as the Academy had put it. In China, the foremost authoritarian power on the planet, this should have de facto placed Alexievich in the category of 'sensitive'—politically problematic—authors.

For a Western mind like mine, an opponent of the totalitarian system should be persona non grata in the Middle Kingdom, be she Belarusian or Russian. But, disconcertingly, this was clearly not the logic at play. The reason was simple; there was no contradiction here: the

Chinese censors did not see *Second-Hand Time* as a compendium of testaments on the collapse of a world. Rather, they saw in it a nostalgic rendering, tinged with emotion and regret, of a lost country: the Union of Soviet Socialist Republics (USSR), China's former 'big brother'.

It is perhaps unnecessary to point out that for the leaders of the Chinese regime, the fall of the Soviet empire in 1991 was a disaster as well as traumatic. Now that the country is the world's second largest economic power and Washington's greatest rival, this memory has become a scenario that must be averted. In Europe it is difficult to imagine how much attention the Chinese pay to analysing the Soviet collapse, hoping to avoid getting caught in a similar deadly spiral. How to reform without falling in turn? This is the number one question facing Xi Jinping. In the 1950s, the refrain was 'the USSR of today is the China of tomorrow'; for him, it is now something like: 'the USSR of yesterday absolutely must not become the China of tomorrow'.

Before he came to office, some Chinese liberals thought they saw in Xi a possible Mikhail Gorbachev, the Soviet leader who launched the 1980s reform (*perestroika*) and transparency (*glasnost*) policies that would precipitate the fall of the Soviet Union. A few months before his nomination as general secretary of the Chinese Communist Party, Xi Jinping had engaged with those considered to be reformers. He had spoken on several occasions with the economist Hu Deping. As well as being close to Xi and another 'prince's son', Hu is the eldest son of the reformer Hu Yaobang, whose death in 1989 had provoked the ill-fated pro-democracy demonstrations. And wasn't Xi similar in many ways to Gorbachev—a relatively young politician, part of the inner circle, compelled by circumstance to make important changes?

In October 2012, a group of Chinese intellectual reformers (some living in exile in the United States, others flying in from China) met in New York for a meeting on the future of their country. The imminent transition of power from Hu Jintao to Xi Jinping was of course at the heart of the discussion. Pin Ho, manager of the dissident site Minjing, made his predictions: 'If Xi Jinping does not introduce political reform, there will be a coup'. Yao Jianfu, a Party veteran turned dissident, was more reserved, and warned against wishful thinking.

At the end of Xi's first mandate in 2018, it could be said that history has proved Yao Jianfu right. But, in their defence, the intellectuals were not the only ones who mistook their reformist dreams for reality. The journalists were also too quick to dub Xi the 'Chinese Gorbachev'. A veteran BBC journalist, John Simpson, admitted to having felt *déjà vu* in Beijing on Xi's appointment as Party leader in 2012. During the eighteenth Party Congress in November of that year, which marked the start of the Xi era, Simpson was reminded of

Moscow in 1988, when he had been in the USSR to cover an important Soviet Communist Party meeting. Everything in 2012 Beijing reminded him of the moment when Gorbachev made the decisions that would lead to the end of the Soviet regime. And this sufficed to persuade Simpson that Xi Jinping was on the cusp of leading China into a 'radical change' towards democratisation. The liberals had not managed to implement such change in the 1980s, discarded and forgotten after the bloody repression of the Tiananmen democratic movement in 1989. Was it now to be achieved by this young leader, less heavy-handed in style than his predecessors? 'Can Xi reform the system, without—like Gorbachev—destroying it?' Simpson wrote in *The Guardian* a few months later. 'He has advantages that Gorbachev lacked, so it's not absolutely impossible. But I suspect things have gone too far for traditional Marxism-Leninism to survive.' Also at this time, the fall of neo-Maoist and anti-liberal hardliner Bo Xilai, following accusations of corruption, seemed to attest to the Party's will to reform.

Since then, however, Xi has defied expectations. Some expected a Chinese Gorbachev, and got a Chinese Putin instead. He proved it in spring 2018, when he decided to revise the Constitution so as to lift presidential term limits. With this move, 'China stepped from autocracy into dictatorship. That was when Xi Jinping, already the world's most powerful man, let it be known that he will change China's constitution so that he can rule as president for as long as he chooses—and conceivably for life,' announced *The Economist*'s editorial on 1 March 2018. No Chinese leader since Mao has been so powerful. Even before this personal coup, the way Xi dealt with the case of 2010 Nobel Prize winner Liu Xiaobo, terminally ill with cancer, showed the extent of his determination to bring dissenting intellectuals into line. Sentenced in 2009 to eleven years' imprisonment for subversion of state power, Liu, who had already been incarcerated for his participation in the Tiananmen democratic movement, was one of the more virulent critics of the regime, constantly denouncing the communist government. Transferred to hospital following the deterioration in his health, he died in July 2017 aged 61, the Chinese authorities having denied requests for his transfer abroad. This intransigence contrasted with the period when Beijing, under pressure from Western governments, agreed to release dissidents on medical grounds, such as Wei Jingsheng in 1997 and Wang Dan a year later.

Xi's 'radical reform' was more of a return to the past and, as we shall see, conceived under the aegis of Mao Zedong, founder of the regime. Gorbachev is not a role model for Xi; if anything, he rejects him. Perhaps, then, we should diagnose and treat the 'Gorbachev Syndrome' that has wreaked such havoc among mistaken and misled journalists. Since the fall of the Soviet bloc, each new Chinese leader has been identified as the one to radically reform the political system. And yet, on each occasion, these expectations are dashed. To be compared with Gorbachev is the best way to thwart one's career prospects within the Party, for any inclination towards reform is associated with softness at a time of nationalist renewal. In the words of Minxin Pei, a Sino-American Chinese politics expert, 'It is like having a huge target drawn on your chest.'

Hu Jintao, general secretary of the Party between 2002 and 2012, had kept many guessing for a relatively long time as to the nature of his intentions. With Xi Jinping, however, a few weeks sufficed to dispel any uncertainty regarding his. At the end of 2012, on one of his first trips as the newly-appointed general secretary, he visited Shenzhen, in the south, where his father had supervised implementation of the economic reforms launched by Deng Xiaoping. Xi placed a wreath at the foot of the Great Helmsman's statue overlooking the city, a former fishing village turned dynamic metropolis and a symbol of the three decades of China's economic boom.

Shenzhen had also been Deng's destination three years after the Tiananmen repression, to signal to the conservatives in the Party that reforms and opening up had not been abandoned. The liberals immediately saw Xi's gesture as proof that he had decided to go down the road of political reform. They were mistaken. It was also during this trip that he started to caution Party members: China had to learn the lesson of the fall of the

Soviet Union. For several months, this speech was not made public. Xi gave it internally to the Party on several occasions. For instance, on 5 January 2013, he asked the new permanent and alternative members of the Central Committee,

> Why did the Soviet Union collapse? Why did the Soviet Communist Party lose its power? One of the main reasons is that the ideological struggle was intense, that the history of the USSR and of the CPSU had been completely denied, that Lenin had been rejected, as was Stalin, and that historical nihilism had run its course. Ideological confusion was everywhere. Almost no Party organ on any level had been of any use. The army wasn't under the control of the Party. Finally, the Communist Party of the Soviet Union, which was nevertheless a great party, was dissolved like a flock of sparrows. The Soviet Union, which had been a great socialist country, collapsed. This is the lesson we must learn from the errors of the past!

The medium of choice for this lesson was a documentary. In 2013, all over the country, Party members were invited to private viewings of a curious film. Not one of those big 'Hollywood' productions the Party had become keen on, such as *The Founding of the Republic*, which was released in 2009 to celebrate the sixtieth anniversary of the People's Republic of China, featuring a cast of over 100 famous actors. Instead, this was a three-hour didactic documentary entitled *In Memory of the Collapse of the Communist Party and the Soviet Union*. Shot in early 2012, the film was devised by the Party's Central Commission for Discipline Inspection (CCDI) and the Research Centre for World Socialism of the Academy of Social Sciences.

The film crew had travelled to Russia to interview witnesses, who happened mostly to be former Soviet Communist Party members. Oddly enough, they were all desperately nostalgic for the USSR's lost greatness. In the film, a voice-over recites a ponderous political analysis tinged with a hint of paranoia, characteristic of authoritarian regimes. The original sin, it explains, can be traced back to the Twentieth Congress of the Communist Party of the Soviet Union on 25 February 1956, during which Khrushchev gave his 'secret speech' before 1,430 delegates. This was when the seeds of disaster had been sown. The Soviets had started to burn down their idols: Stalin, but also Lenin, which opened the floodgates to a questioning of Marxist faith. Gorbachev, father of the 1980s reforms, and his 'accomplices'—Alexander Yakovlev, Edward Shevardnadze, and Boris Yeltsin—were all 'children of the Twentieth Congress'. In a nutshell, they were traitors. When they came to power, their objective had been to bring down socialism and communism. Under the influence of Western powers, who were counting on them, they had implemented their destructive policies: the introduction of a multi-party system, the authorisation of NGOs, the liberalisation of the media, the abandonment of control over means of production, the privatisation of public industries, and severing the link between the Party and the army.

The documentary specifically demonises Gorbachev and accuses him of selling himself to the Americans. Weak in his decision-making, ideologically hesitant, he had driven his country to ruin through a wave of privatisations. The wealth of a huge majority of the people had been collected by a handful of oligarchs from the old Party bureaucracy. It was the beginning of the reign of violence and of the mafia. The final blow came with the former USSR falling victim to separatist movements. Twenty years after the fall of the motherland of socialism, the outcome of *glasnost* and *perestroika* was not just negative—it was downright criminal.

The film ends with the usual elements of propaganda: not all is lost for communism, since China has taken up the baton. Gennady Zyuganov, leader since 1993 of what's left of the Russian Communist Party, drives this point home in his interview with the Beijing film crew:

> In the space of thirty years, China has achieved formidable results. I hope you will not forget the reasons for the collapse of the USSR and the lessons of the fall of the Communist Party of the Soviet Union: only by [learning these lessons] can the Chinese people build their own country.

The documentary ends with images of the Kremlin set to *The Internationale*. The voiceover gives some closing recommendations to Party members: never renounce socialism and Marxism; never give in to the influence of 'hostile forces' who wish to 'Westernise' the country and 'sow the seeds of separatism'. Beware above all of 'the manoeuvres of Western powers', of their 'financial and ideological manipulations', of their use of NGOs, of 'their will to incite chaos by promoting governance from the streets'.

With this film, the tone was set from the first year of Xi's mandate: the West was the enemy and Gorbachev had been its puppet. Xi, on the other hand, would be a herald of Chinese Marxism-Leninism. But in avoiding becoming a new Gorbachev, some worry that he could well become a new Brezhnev instead, given Xi's questioning of the rules put in place by Deng Xiaoping in 1982, which included the presidential two-term limit. These regulations, designed to avoid the rise of a 'new Mao' and the bloodthirsty excesses of an autocracy, had allowed a renewal and rejuvenation of the Party leadership—particularly those imposing an age limit on important offices. Xi has subverted them in order to place his allies in strategic roles. According to Jérôme Doyon, Associate Researcher at the European Council on Foreign Relations (ECFR) and chief editor of the journal *China Analysis*, 'if these rules are revoked and the officials given the impression that they can stay in power for longer, then the situation could become problematic. Namely for the younger members who wish to come to power.' In the Soviet Union, Brezhnev revoked the rejuvenation policy launched by Khrushchev, laying the foundations for what was to become a gerontocracy. Will Xi succumb to the same temptation? Is he leading the Communist Party down a slippery slope?

3

SON OF THE YELLOW EARTH

'When I grow up, I want to be president ... This is the dream of many kids around the world. However, the path towards achieving this dream can be vastly different from country to country...' This anonymous video, about five minutes long, became a hit in China when it was posted and widely disseminated on the Internet at the end of 2013. Available in both Chinese and English versions, the lively educational cartoon aimed at children outlined three political systems found in the world today—with the Chinese system emerging as the winner. The studio behind *How Are Leaders Made?* is called Renewal Road—the Xi regime's favourite slogan.

The United States, the leading world power, Britain, one of Europe's greatest democracies, and China are described in turn. The protagonists are Barack Obama, David Cameron, and Xi Jinping, but only the latter is referred to by name—red *noblesse oblige*. First, how does one become president of the United States? The path 'sounds easy', we are told:

Anyone born on American soil, who has lived in the States for more than fourteen years, and is now over thirty-five years old, can run for president. ... But pulling it off is a super-complex business [here the register becomes more informal to sound more 'hip']. You need first to set up a team and choose your running-mate, then deliver speeches, fight through debates, raise funds wherever you can, and beat all opponents to finally sit in the Oval Office. The whole business lasts over one year. Without a glib tongue, extraordinary stamina, and most importantly an unending flow of greenbacks, no-one can ever pull it off. The two candidates in the 2012 US presidential election spent a total of US$2.04 billion. Alas, becoming a 'political hero' is definitely far more difficult than becoming an 'American idol'!

Of course, this now seems ironic; the cartoon was made before Donald Trump, a real estate tycoon who rose to fame through reality television, was elected president at the end of 2016. But back to the cartoon.

The next example is Great Britain. The character representing the then prime minister, David Cameron, needs to take leadership of his party and obtain a majority in the House of Commons, but 'That chance is way narrower than Susan Boyle's chance of winning *Britain's Got Talent*.' Finally comes China. There, one encounters a truly exemplary 'meritocracy'. Take Xi Jinping, the commentator says:

He started at a primary-level office, one similar to local councils in the West. Later he was promoted to run a county, then a city, and then different provinces like Fujian and Zhejiang and Shanghai. He went on to become the 'veep', and finally the Party general secretary, and president.

What a career, and what a man! 'He experienced sixteen major job transfers, and governed an accumulative population of over 150 million over forty plus years', before—of course—seeing to the wellbeing of 1.3 billion Chinese citizens as leader of the Chinese Communist Party. 'In this system, before a party member could take the helm of China, he would have navigated all kinds of rapids and shoals. More importantly, he would have participated in the deliberation and formulation of many major strategies and policies.'

Xi's predecessors parade on screen: Mao Zedong, Deng Xiaoping, Jiang Zemin, and Hu Jintao. The commentary continues: 'That is why over the decades, through several leadership transitions, China has managed to keep its policies generally consistent, and worked along one national development strategy. This is one of the secrets of the "Chinese Miracle". ... Many roads lead to national leadership, and every country has one for itself. Whether by a single ballot that gets the whole nation out to vote, or by meritocratic screening that requires years of hard work, like the making of a kung fu master. As long as the people are satisfied, and the country develops and progresses as a result, it's working.'

The video glosses over problematic leadership transitions, such as those following the death of Mao and the toppling of the Gang of Four, or the events of 2012 just before Xi's accession to power, when his rival Bo Xilai attempted a 'coup' with the support of other high officials. *How Are Leaders Made?* is a glorification of the 'Chinese model', one that is based on experience and guarantees security, as opposed to Western democracy, governed by money and the vagaries of open elections; Beijing's solid meritocracy versus the fragile oligarchies of Washington or London; the Beijing Consensus, and not the Washington Consensus, one might say.

This discourse is more than simple propaganda. It is doctrine theorised and taught at the Central Party School since the 1980s. At the time, the regime found in the city-state of Singapore a source of inspiration and a model of a 'Productive and efficient state led by an elite administration.' In his memoirs, Lee Kuan Yew, the Chinese-origin founder of Singapore, expressed his admiration for the Middle Kingdom:

> Everyone has a file or dossier, which starts with his primary school report, containing not only his academic performance but his teachers' assessments of his character, behaviour, values and attitudes. At every stage of his career, there are records of judgements of his peers and superiors. At every level for promotion, all suitable candidates are assessed before appointment. At the top echelons of the pyramid is a core between 5,000 and

10,000 who have been chosen and carefully graded by the organisation department ['Human Resources Department'] of the Communist Party, not the government. To ensure that gradings are correct, inspection teams from the centre visit provinces and cities to assess the assessors and interview a cadre before he is promoted. In case of disagreement, the matter would be reviewed in Beijing. The selection process is thorough, searching and comprehensive.

This non-democratic co-optation model is one defended by many Asian and even some Western intellectuals. This is the case of Daniel Bell, a renowned Canadian political scientist based at the prestigious Tsinghua University. He has long advocated a political system that follows China's Confucian tradition and, in his opinion, some elements are already in place. For instance, the Party, with its 86 million members, is not comparable to its Western counterparts, nor is it a monolithic political formation. On the contrary, Bell sees in it a pluralistic organisation made up of members of different groups selected for their potential to represent the whole country. In fact, he proposes it be renamed the 'Chinese Meritocratic Union' (*Zhongguo xianneng lianmeng*). This fascination with the finely-tuned Party machine is not so distant from the Jesuits' admiration for the 'celestial bureaucracy', the mandarin caste, between the sixteenth and eighteenth centuries.

The idea of progressive and rational ascent towards the highest functions of power is not just marketing spin. It is both the cornerstone of the Chinese model and its justification. But is Xi Jinping truly the perfect illustration of this 'meritocracy', as *How Are Leaders Made?* implied?

That Xi did indeed start off quite low down the hierarchy is undeniable, even if in truth he was put there by the regime. What the propaganda machine has turned into a significant feat—reaching the top of the hierarchy starting from nothing—glosses over the trials and tribulations involved. Xi was sent to the countryside during the Cultural Revolution, where he endured difficult conditions. Before that he was a well-off Beijing schoolboy. In 1968, to put an end to the chaos he had himself brought about, Mao had decided to empty the cities of their youth and send them out amongst the peasants to be re-educated. 'I studied at the university of green forests, that is where I learned something,' he said in 1964, relaunching a 1950s movement known as *shangshan xiaxiang* ('go up the mountains, go down to the countryside').

The directive that would affect Xi and millions of other students was read out on the radio on a winter evening in 1968, 21 December, and published the next day in the *People's Daily* (*Renmin Ribao*):

> It is absolutely necessary for educated youth to go to the countryside to get re-educated by the poor and lower-middle peasants. We must persuade the officials and other inhabitants of the cities to send their children who are graduates of secondary schools and uni-

versities to the countryside. There should be an effort to mobilise. The comrades from all the rural areas should welcome these youths.

Xi Jinping was fifteen at the time and got caught up in the movement. It was an exodus on an unprecedented scale in the country's history, affecting about 17 million people in total. The same scenes were witnessed throughout the country: columns of young people heading towards the stations, to the rhythm of revolutionary chants and songs; the outpourings of enthusiasm; the farewells; the welcoming committees on their arrival in the country; and then the billeting. Those who left in 1968 or 1969 were keen to go. Many, like Xi, volunteered. And this decision was to prove fundamental to his intellectual development.

'I remember clearly the special train that took us to Shaanxi,' he said in a 2004 televised interview, giving a rare account of his youth:

> It was in January 1969. Everyone was crying. I was laughing. My family, who had accompanied me to the train had asked why, and I told them, 'I'd cry if I wasn't leaving. How can I be sure that I have a future here? So don't cry.' And then, their tears turned to laughter.

The young Xi was happy to escape the stifling political atmosphere of the city. In those troubled times, when one had always to demonstrate ever purer revolutionary zeal, his 'family history' worked against him.

His father had been the victim of a political purge and ousted in 1962.

Xi Zhongxun, born in 1913, was an important figure—a hero of the Revolution, one of Mao's companions, a comrade since the early days in Shaanxi province. But this did not protect him in the 1960s from accusations of belonging to an 'anti-Party' clique, after his protector, Gao Gang, general secretary of the Party Central Committee, was disgraced. Mao enjoyed inventing enemies for himself in a state of permanent revolution. Overnight, Xi Senior was branded a 'class enemy' and his family fell from an enviable status as members of a privileged caste—revolutionaries and their families—to life as 'purged' outcasts. Four years later, during the Cultural Revolution, his son became the perfect target: 'I was told, "You deserve to be shot a hundred times!" I thought that there was no difference between being shot once and being shot a hundred times. Why should I be afraid of that threat?' he would muse years later. Yet, in the commotion, he had been sequestered by the Red Guards in the Central Party School, where his mother had taken refuge. This was not Xi Jinping's most glorious moment, and was an episode that threatened his fierce desire to avoid being branded a 'bad element'. When a father is chastised, there are two types of son: those who avenge them, and those who atone for them. Xi belongs to the second category. He has always sought to erase the mark left on him by his father's faults. And so, the teenage Xi left Beijing. He requested to go to northern China, to a village near Yan'an. He had heard his family mention the place: it was there that his father had headed a combat base at the beginning of the Revolution, in the 1930s. The region, now called 'Yellow Earth' after the colour of its loess soil, is considered the cradle of Chinese civilisation. With its cave-houses (*yaodong*), it is redolent of the ancestral era of the Yellow Emperor, the mythical founder of Chinese civilisation 5,000 years ago.

The loess plateaux are also legendary in Revolutionary folklore for having been Mao's stronghold before his 1949 victory; the communist leader and his comrades had sought refuge in this bare land from the pursuing Nationalist troops. There are many famous photographs of Mao in his padded jacket, standing before a cave or writing inside his refuge. In other words, for the Chinese people, this yellow earth is a site of collective memory, and Xi Jinping would use that to his advantage. Put simply, his sojourn in the region allowed him to link big—imperial—history to both Revolutionary history and his own family history.

The first months were difficult. 'We were there temporarily, to get away from Beijing, and did not think we had to fit in with the people. We were not accustomed nor adapted to the place,' Xi admitted. An anecdote illustrates the distance between this urban youth and the local peasants:

I have often been asked about this story: I had fed the dogs bread. ... It was a misunderstanding really. I did not think I was wasting food. I had kept the bread too long, it was dry. And when I was going through my bag, I found some, and so I put it aside to feed to the dogs that used to come to my door. When the people saw me do that, they asked me what it was I was feeding the dogs, and I told them it was bread. They had never eaten nor seen bread before. Soon the story spread by word-of-mouth throughout the whole county: 'Ah, those educated youth who feed the dogs bread, they are so unseemly!'

Such misunderstandings were not the sole source of discomfort. The living conditions were difficult. Xi lived in a cave-house dug out of the yellow earth. A young city-dweller, he had never been subjected to fleas, but they are omnipresent in this region during the summer. Xi felt he was sleeping on a mattress infested with vermin. The food was also different from what he had been used to. Instead of rice and wheat, he had to content himself with less refined cereals. He was bored, did not take to, and did not see the point in, working in the fields. Three months after his arrival, he returned to Beijing. But he was arrested and sentenced to a spell of re-education through labour. He dug trenches for water pipes in a Beijing neighbourhood. He eventually returned to the village of Liangjiahe on his family's advice. Did he want to end up a delinquent on the run?

This time around, the young Xi adjusted to country life and settled in:

> In their writings, authors speak of the tragic fate of the educated youth but that was not my experience. I was only miserable in the beginning, but little by little I adapted to the local lifestyle, and especially after having completely integrated the masses, I felt on the contrary that I was fulfilling myself.

This transformation is key to understanding Xi Jinping's career. He still refers to it today as the founding event of his political life. In Seattle in 2015, addressing an American audience, he embellished this concrete and daily connection with the peasants 'who lived in caves dug into the earth'. This period came across as a fundamental part of his personal narrative. When he addressed journalists from the BRICS countries (Brazil, Russia, India, China, and South Africa) at a summit in 2013, he insisted:

> In the current system, officials are selected step by step. If you take my case, for instance, I worked in the countryside as Party secretary to a production brigade, and then I worked at the county level, the municipal level, the provincial, and the central level successively. Officials who have a lot of field experience know how to see the bigger picture, and show an awareness of national realities and the people's demands.

Xi also uses this tactic with Chinese audiences. With a hint of megalomania, he declared in a 2004 television interview that the village had needed him and was part of him. 'I felt at home there; it allowed me to endure attacks even at the height of the Cultural Revolution. Several struggle sessions took place in the villages in northern Shaanxi against Liu Shaoqi's and Deng Xiaoping's local representatives.' He added lucidly that 'the locals were good to me, for I was in my father's former military base. At only nineteen he had been the head of the Shaanxi-Gansu borderlands soviet. So as a result many people protected me, and taught me how to cope, which made me stronger.'

In a long text written in 2002, Xi Jinping conceptualised this fundamental experience as having fostered in him a 'yellow earth attachment' (*huang tudi qingjie*), or 'yellow earth complex'. For Xi, what lurks beneath this nebula of representations and emotions is the importance of one's connection with the 'masses'—the usual communist gloss, one might say—and of pragmatism and self-confidence. 'When I encounter a problem, I know it has a solution,' he writes. Self-confidence and the ability to face challenges are qualities he has indeed shown, and which explain his successful career. 'I arrived in the yellow earth when I was fifteen, I was lost, indecisive; when I left aged twenty-two, I had clear life-goals and self-confidence. The northern plateaux of Shaanxi province are my roots as a servant of the State. It was there that my unwavering ideal to devote myself to the people was born. Wherever I go, I will always be a son of the yellow earth.' It makes for quite the mission statement.

It was also at this time that Xi first manifested his leadership skills. The poor and rough locals grew to accept him:

> The people saw that I had begun to change, my relationship with them improved. My house gradually became the centre of village life. Every evening, young and old would stop by. I would show them my books, talk to them about places and periods they knew nothing of. They wanted to hear about the type of things the city-dwellers spoke about and which they did not understand. Even the local Party Secretary ended up coming to see me for a chat. In his eyes, we young people were more knowledgeable and possessed a better understanding of things. I also gained quite a reputation in the village. I was only about sixteen or seventeen, and yet the elders would come to see me if there was a problem.

The 'yellow earth complex', then, is a deep anchoring force for Xi Jinping, in Mao's wake. Like the Great Helmsman, he can pride himself on his extensive knowledge of poor rural China—unlike his predecessor, Hu Jintao, whose career was that of a typical Party apparatchik. This is a major advantage for Xi, who can claim to be of the masses and not seem detached from their reality. It allows him to reconcile the 'nobility' of his rank as a 'son of' with his acquaintance with the humblest of his people.

Xi's Shaanxi experience also confers yet another opportune advantage. It indicates that he was a victim of the madness of the Cultural Revolution, rather than being one of the young Red Guards who carried it out, an unpleasant memory for many Chinese people. This gives him quite an edge, even if he does not boast about it. During the same period, his future political rival Bo Xilai, another 'son of', took part in the Red Guards' abuse as a squadron leader in Beijing.

Conversely, Xi Jinping had to apply eight times before being accepted into the Communist Youth League, and ten times before becoming a member of the Party. His bad 'family history' was regularly given as a reason for this. He describes how, after having filled in his first application to the Youth League, he had invited his production brigade's Party secretary to dinner to request that he transmit the application. The latter expressed his reservations: 'What can you do? Upstairs they all say that you are a child that needs to be educated. ... They say that you have not distanced yourself enough [from your father, an enemy of the Party].' Xi stood his ground, and pointed out that there was no official document outlining his father's sentence:

> Where is the verdict against my father? When a fault is committed, there is a verdict. But where is the one against my father? Did you obtain the documents from the central government? If not, then convey my request. Who do you think I am? What have I done? Have I

written or chanted counter-revolutionary slogans? I am a young man who wants to build a career. What is the problem with that?

His obstinacy would pay off. No one would forget that he had been a victim, along with many Chinese citizens, of the Mao-era abuses.

Xi is the first of this generation of 'educated youth' sent to the countryside to come to power. They are known as the *chiku* generation, the generation who 'tasted bitterness', who suffered the most. Li Keqiang, Xi's prime minister, and Wang Qishan, the head of anti-corruption during Xi's first term, also belong to this generation. Their age group has a slightly unique status within the Chinese population: during their forced exodus, they had encountered first-hand the true misery of the Chinese peasantry. Many suffered from this experience; others were disillusioned by it. In the countryside, they discovered the lies of the regime, and some decided no longer to support it; they became dissidents. Such was the case of Cai Chongguo, one of the former leaders of the Tiananmen democratic movement, whom I met in Hong Kong, where he now lives in exile following a long stay in France. The two-and-a-half years he spent among the peasants opened his eyes and reinforced his independent-mindedness. When he was not working, he would peruse three books stolen for him by his best friend: Karl Marx and Friedrich Engels' *The German Ideology*; *The French Revolution*, by early-twentieth-century French Marxist historian Albert Mathiez; and Hegel's *Shorter Logic*.

> Marx's reasoning seemed more profound to me, for there is a logic to it, both of which are missing from Mao's texts in my view. This was made particularly clear to me when I read *The German Ideology*, which made me realise that Mao was not a Marxist, for he spent his time lecturing others on morality.

If we believe his own account, Xi Jinping, too, spent a lot of his free time in the countryside reading. Once he even travelled tens of kilometres on foot to purchase a copy of Goethe's *Faust*. This is how he portrayed himself, in October 2014, before artists and writers at a forum on literature and art in Beijing—an obvious replica of Mao's 1942 Yan'an Forum on Literature and Art. 'When I was in a village in the north of Shaanxi Province, I heard that an educated youth had a copy of *Faust*, and so I walked 15 kilometres to borrow that book, then I walked the same 15 kilometres again to return it to him.' Unfortunately, the president did not say what he had thought of it; but, unlike Cai Chongguo, books did not lead Xi to rebel against the regime—quite the opposite. His experience in the countryside led him to sign a deal, not with the Devil, but with the Party.

Unsurprisingly, Yellow Earth has become a staple of propaganda speeches in the Xi era. There is no better way to depict the leader as a humble man close to his people, and especially as a pure man. Insisting on his rootedness—never missing a chance to remind his audience that he carries that land within him—Xi seems to promote his 'native' status. He is a Chinese man from the heart of the country, born again in this hinterland, and anchored in the long history of Chinese civilisation—that of Yellow Emperor, and of Mao. It is a well-orchestrated pastoral myth. Propaganda readily refers to the 'spirit of the cave' in reference to this golden age from which Xi seems to have emerged. The cave-houses of the yellow earth are the equivalent of log cabins to American presidents. Xi, on his pilgrimages there, can evoke his close—and real—ties to this cradle of Chinese civilisation. The plain-living native son can boast of his frugality, in contrast to the voracity of the nouveau riche; of inner China, in contrast to the coastal regions perverted by monetary greed; of a China of great men, in contrast to Western decadence.

In fact, Xi exploits this legendary past in his fight against corruption. To counter excesses, he gladly harks back to the early days of Maoism. This moment of Revolutionary history following the Long March, when Mao's troops set up camp in China's loess soil, is referred to on a near-pathological rolling basis in propaganda speeches. In autumn 2016, an official documentary on Xi's fight against corruption recalled the 'conversation in a cave-house' (*yaodongdui*) that took place in July 1945 between Mao and Huang Yanpei, leader of the 'middle-way' China Democratic League. How, Huang asked, to escape the law of cyclical history, this curse that inevitably condemns a government first to succeed, then to fall? Mao replied: 'We've already discovered a new path. We can break out of this cycle. This new path belongs to the people. The government will only avoid becoming complacent if it is under the supervision of the people. If everyone takes responsibility, a good system of governance will prevail.'

Xi still finds validity in this analysis dating back to the early days of Chinese communism. He is convinced that purer and more honest officials who are close to the masses can save the Party and stop it from falling as did the Communist Party of the Soviet Union. It would be a mistake to take this as mere cynicism. Xi deeply believes that the return to original Maoism is the only way to save China's future. It is one of the symptoms of his 'yellow earth complex': history haunts him, for in it he believes he will find the key to facing the future.

Since coming to office, Xi has constantly referred back to Mao in the 1930s; the Mao who issued the 'Three Rules of Discipline' for the soldiers of the People's Liberation Army (PLA)—(1) Obey orders in your actions; (2) Don't take anything from the workers and peasants; and (3) Turn in all things taken from local bullies—and the 'Eight Points of Attention' (Put back the doors you have taken down for bed-boards; put back the straw you have used for bedding; speak politely; pay fairly for what you buy; return everything you borrow; pay for anything you damage; don't bathe within sight of women; only defecate in the latrines). All things being equal, Xi insists that these rules should be taken as a model.

A few months after his nomination as general secretary of the Party in 2012, he issued new rules. The 'Eight-Point Regulation', also known as the 'Eight-Point Rules' (*baguiding*), were presented in late 2012 during a Politburo meeting. These were rules not for soldiers, but for Party officials. Leaders first need to stay in touch with 'real people', Xi asserted, through regular personal visits to regions affected by social issues: 'Inspection tours which are a mere formality should be strictly prohibited.' During such visits, there must be no 'no welcome banner, no red carpet, no floral arrangement or grand receptions for officials'. Politburo members should only take part in inauguration ceremonies with permission from the Central Committee. There must be no more useless lustre, but instead a return to a kind of simplicity, and above all efficiency. Official meetings should be shortened and 'be free of empty-talk and blather'—something of a hallmark of the regime. Paperwork should be cut down, and there should be an end, too, to the mobilisation of students and other Chinese abroad to welcome visiting officials arriving at foreign airports. These visiting officials should also be accompanied by smaller entourages. There should be less disturbance to traffic when leaders travel by car, so as to avoid inconvenience to the public. Finally, the media should seek to reduce the number of news reports related to members of the Politburo.

So many virtuous regulations! Their impact is not easily measured, but an outline of Xi's intellectual and political perspective can clearly be sketched from his explicit references to a founding episode of 'correct' behaviour. After the somewhat drab rigidity of his predecessor, Xi has exploited his personal history to impose a new style and a new faith. Readily captured on camera amidst the people, the son of the yellow earth believes it is possible to get back to one's roots.

The 'Red Princes', of whom Xi is the illustrious representative, would lose everything in the event of democratisation—for obvious political reasons, but also for economic ones. Many are businessmen. They either occupy senior positions in private or state-owned companies, or take advantage of their supposed influence to act as intermediaries. As Steve Dickinson, a China-based American lawyer specialising in fraud cases, put it in 2014, 'What's the point of running the Communist Party if you can't get a couple billion for your family?' Many relatives of 'Red Princes' were implicated by the Panama Papers leaked in 2015, including Xi Jinping's brother-in-law—an inconvenient revelation to emerge during the battle against corruption. Following the release of the Papers, Beijing denounced the revelations as no more than foreign attacks motivated by a political agenda. The pro-government *Global Times* wrote: 'The

Western media has taken control of the interpretation each time there has been such a document dump, and Washington has demonstrated particular influence in it. Information that is negative to the US can always be minimised, while exposure of non-Western leaders, such as Putin, can get extra spin.' Meanwhile, the Chinese authorities blocked the websites of foreign media that had published the investigations.

In short, like the other members of the Red nobility, Xi Jinping, who has never directly been exposed, may not stand to benefit from greater transparency in China, nor from the upheaval of economic reform. He is probably also quite critical of the record of his predecessor Hu, who, in the eyes of the aristocrats of the communist regime, lacked the type of firm-handedness that reassures the wealthy; nor have they hesitated to say so. In 2011, Zhang Musheng, whose father was Zhou Enlai's secretary, sparked controversy with *Transform our Cultural Perspective*, a pamphlet arguing against Hu's policies. In Zhang's opinion, the unprecedented explosion of inequality and corruption that China was witnessing needed to be brought under proper control. Otherwise, the Party would lose its legitimacy. What was needed was a fresh start: a 'new democracy', a concept of national unity bringing together communists and 'patriotic capitalists'. Mao had put forward this idea in the 1940s before coming to power and subsequently abandoning it. The current crisis, Zhang argued, urged a rethink of the alliance between political and economic forces, but still an alliance under the control of a strong state. The pamphlet's preface was written by General Liu Yuan, son of President Liu Shaoqi, who fell foul of and died under the Cultural Revolution in 1969. The general sang the praises of strength: 'Military culture is Humanity's oldest and most important wisdom.' One could not wish for greater clarity.

Can we find in texts of this kind the broad strokes of the programme Xi would come to embody? After all, he is seeking to reconnect with the spirit of the 'new democracy' and to consolidate the Party-State. For instance, the philosopher Zhang Boshu of Columbia University claims that there is a worrying proximity between the propositions of the 'Red Princes' and Xi's own line. Notably, he is not a target for their public criticisms.

There is another important link, one of a more intellectual nature: that between Xi and both the 'Neo-Maoists' and the 'New Left'. These two movements, which share similar tendencies, have both been on the rise since Xi came to power. The more authoritarian of the two, the Neo-Maoists, were recently put in charge of the last reformists' journal to have survived, *Yanhuang Chunqiu* (China Through the Ages). Xi has particularly nurtured them after having deposed their hero. Almost immediately after he came to power, he condemned Bo Xilai to life imprisonment for corruption. In the southwest city of Chongqing, where he had been Party secretary since 2007, Bo was leading a policy summed up in four characters: *chang hong da hei*, 'sing red and strike the black [the mafia in China]'.

Bo rehabilitated Neo-Maoist folklore, whilst launching economic policies aimed at tackling inequalities; he had also officially made the fight against corruption his top priority, making his story truly one of someone hoisted by their own petard. The Neo-Maoist and New Left intellectuals praised this 'Chongqing Model' at the time, and saw in it the future of national politics. They were not completely mistaken, since Xi took the idea for himself. The same intellectuals who were enamoured with Bo before his downfall have now made Xi the object of their affections. The political scientist Li Weidong believes that the president, 'an unconditional Mao fan' (*shendu maofen*), is 'following Bo Xilai's political line without Bo Xilai' (*Meiyou Bo Xilai de Bo Xilai luxian*).

The Neo-Maoists have not been the only ones to take comfort in Xi's leadership. The 'chairman of everything' also appeals to the Neo-Authoritarian movement, a school of thought that flourished after the suppression of the Tiananmen democratic movement in 1989. Xiao Gongqin, professor of history at the East China Normal University and a Neo-Authoritarian figurehead, shares most of Xi's political beliefs, which shows how fluid they can be. Xiao argues that Xi is not an unconditional Maoist, but rather has the potential to save the country from falling into one of two extremes: either a right-wing 'colour revolution' calling for a democratic and constitutional system similar to that of the United States, or a form of left-wing extremism dreaming of a return to the Cultural Revolution. Xiao is therefore delighted with Xi's presidency, which he terms 'Neo-Authoritarianism 2.0'.

At the end of 2013, during a debate organised by Hong Kong's Phoenix television channel, Xiao explained that China was in need of 'reform with an iron fist' (*tiewan gaige*). In his view, Xi did not suffer from the leftist leanings detected by some, but rather had the ability to 'rule the right using the left':

> When Xi Jinping emphasises ideological governance, it is not a return to a pre-reform era [Maoism] ... With this firm control of ideology, he wishes to avoid an explosive political situation that would destabilise the reforms. The aim is to modernise the governance of the country and Chinese democracy.

In short, Xiao sees Xi as the successor to Deng Xiaoping, father of Chinese communist reform. 'They both represent a version of neo-authoritarianism, for they both wish to keep the Party in power', he claims. And this neo-authoritarianism is a necessary stage for the country's development:

> The final aim is to move towards a more open, more democratic and freer socialist-democratic system. It is a process that may take some time and rely on steady economic development and social change. General

Secretary Xi declared: 'Reforms always create problems but are enhanced by solving them ... The reforms will be endless.' I see these words as demonstrating the capacity of the current Chinese system to adapt and be flexible in its development. China's future is full of hope. We just need to be patient.

Xi needs to apply Mao's methods to reach Deng's objectives; to be Xi by using Deng and Mao; to make something new out of the old—or make something old out of the old, according to sceptics such as the sinologist Sebastian Veg, who believes that China is going through a great ideological revival after years of lying dormant: 'Xi Jinping does not seem to share the prevailing view that to make the State more efficient, Party and ideology must be removed from it', he points out.

Xi's strategy is on the contrary to reaffirm the Party's dominant role as producer of political norms and legitimacy ... The Party becomes a disciplinary tool. The production of Party norms becomes a governing tool ... this evolution can be linked to the ideas of a group of thinkers, mostly legal experts, inspired by Carl Schmitt and other thinkers of authoritarian law, who have been active for the past ten years, especially in the Beijing University Law Faculty, and who are putting forward an alternative to liberal constitutionalism.

This movement includes members of the 'New Left' such as Li Xiaofeng, Gan Yang and Wang Shaoguang, who since the early 2000s have popularised the theories of Carl Schmitt (1888–1985), the German jurist who had been a staunch supporter of the Nazi regime. But there is nothing new or surprising in this appropriation. In Europe, notable left-wing thinkers such as Giorgio Agamben and Étienne Balibar have also borrowed from Schmitt's toolbox to criticise the new global imperialism; Schmitt's axiom being that the law is not an assemblage of norms independent of politics. In Schmitt, Chinese authors have found arguments against liberal conceptions of Western democracy. All's fair in the fight against constitutionalism, and in the Xi era Chinese academics need not fear censorship for deviating from Chinese traditions and straying into the territory of officially despised Western thought.

4

THE MAOIST NATIONAL MYTH

On 3 September 2015, the Chinese regime celebrated the seventieth anniversary of the 'Victories in the Chinese People's War of Resistance Against Japanese Aggression', and the anniversary of the 'Global War Against Fascism'. Xi Jinping proclaimed the day a national holiday to commemorate Japan's defeat in the Second World War. A military procession paraded through the heart of Beijing on Chang'an Avenue, which links the eastern and western sides of the city, and proudly crossed Tiananmen Square. One day, 3 September may also be the date chosen by future historians to mark the start of a new 'Cold War', pitting a nascent empire, China, against a declining superpower, the United States. The show of force was undoubtedly aimed at the Americans, and in the front row of official guests sat Vladimir Putin—a close ally whom Xi honoured with his first state visit abroad in 2013.

Moreover, the Beijing parade appeared to be an exact replica of the one that had taken place in Moscow four months previously, to commemorate Russian heroism during the Second World War. No Western head of state attended festivities in either capital. All had declined the invitation—only France saw fit to send its foreign minister Laurent Fabius to Beijing—either as a sanction against Russia's involvement in Ukraine, or as a refusal to endorse manipulations of history. In the case of China, there was no doubt that the promotion of this victorious day was a sign that Beijing refused to bend to the post-1945 balance of power. In harking back to Japan's past crimes, the Chinese underlined that their neighbour was not the modern democratic country so admired by the West, but indeed the hereditary enemy, the perpetrator of the Nanking Massacre, which resulted, according to Beijing, in 300,000 deaths. The true numbers are said to be lower, but this is the figure quoted by Beijing and circulated worldwide as part of a travelling exhibition. The Japanese and Americans understood that both parade and exhibition were provocations aimed at them. Under authoritarian regimes, military processions are an important element of strategic language—this 3 September parade was worth more than a lengthy speech.

To justify this hostile gesture, Xi Jinping has ostensibly rewritten the events of the Second World War in Asia. He has constantly emphasised the 'resistance' of his people and magnified the Chinese Communist Party's struggle. This manipulation of the facts fools no one. Xi glosses over a key point: the role of Chiang Kai-shek's

Nationalist government. He was the leader of the country at the time, and, consequently, the leader of resistance to the Japanese occupation. This deliberate obscuring of the facts did, in fact, spark controversy a few weeks before the Beijing parade. Posters and trailers of the historical blockbuster film *The Cairo Declaration* showed a majestic Mao attending the November 1943 Cairo Conference beside the American and British leaders, Franklin D. Roosevelt and Winston Churchill, eclipsing his Nationalist enemy. Yet, in reality, it was Chiang Kai-shek who took part in this conference to draw up battle plans against imperialist Japan—not the future founder of communist China, who had retreated to his northern base in Yan'an to plot his rise to power.

China's online community revelled in parodying the poster: over Mao, the figures of various other personalities were Photoshopped, from Mr Bean to the North Korean dictator Kim Jong-un. The film's director, Wen Deguang, claimed the film's media team had made a mistake and stated that Chiang Kai-shek did indeed feature in the film. But the blunder also embarrassed the state media, since it provided enemies of the regime with ammunition. The *Global Times*, the nationalist current's mouthpiece, expressed its concern with 'the historical nihilism and discredit thrown upon Mao Zedong ... which has been in vogue for some time on the internet.'

'Historical nihilism', contrary to what one might think, does not refer to the shameless falsification of history by propaganda. It is in fact quite the opposite. The term describes the total or partial questioning of an episode in the national myth constructed after 1949. Xi Jinping's accession to power did not only correspond with the revival of legendary figures or the return of a Manichean polarisation; as we shall see, it also marked the start of a very concrete and determined political struggle against voices seeking, in the name of historical truth, to fracture the distorted and staid official narrative.

But on 3 September 2015, the online taunts had been forgotten, and Xi Jinping donned Sun Yat-sen's traditional dress, known in the West as the Mao suit; this is the type of clothing that all general secretaries of the Party have worn for such parades. He imparted his vision of history just ahead of the procession exhibiting China's latest missiles, planes and tanks. The victory against Japan, he pointed out, was 'the first complete victory won by China in its resistance against foreign aggression in modern times.' After the humiliation of foreign incursions on its territory from the end of the nineteenth century onwards, after the shame of the unequal treaties, it was Asian power that had emerged victorious—thanks to the Communist Party, which, under Mao's leadership, broke the curse that had stricken the empire for a century.

As the Great Helmsman proclaimed in October 1949 on Tiananmen Square, China had stood up. This is also the image contained in the first verse of the national anthem, *The March of the Volunteers*, which was sung before the start of Xi's speech: 'Arise, ye who refuse to be slaves!' Xi has resolutely adopted this mentality: to remain defiant and hold one's head high, time and again, in the face of yesterday's and today's enemies—starting with Japan, now the Americans' greatest ally in the Asia-Pacific region.

In short, 3 September celebrates the 'great triumph' that 'put an end to China's national humiliation', 'opened up bright prospects for the great renewal of the Chinese nation and set our ancient country on a new journey after achieving rebirth'. In 2015, all was bombast and grandiloquence; 12,000 soldiers were mobilised, and the streets were lined with red flags. Open-top buses transported veterans and their families to the parade on this sunny, late-summer day. At the beginning of his speech, Xi announced:

> On behalf of the Central Committee of the Communist Party of China, the Standing Committee of the National People's Congress, the State Council [the government], the National Committee of the Chinese People's Political Consultative Conference [a rubber-stamp parliamentary body], and the Central Military Commission, I pay high tribute to all the veterans, comrades, patriots and officers in China who took part in the War of Resistance and all the Chinese at home and abroad who contributed significantly to the victory of the War.

Amongst those to whom Xi paid tribute were the descendants of the five martyrs of Mount Langya (Wolf-Tooth Mountain), an episode in the fight against Japanese forces that has always been particularly glorified by the Party. Every Chinese citizen knows the story: in 1941, in the heat of battle, Ma Baoyu, Hu Delin, Hu Fucai, Ge Zhenli and Song Xueyi drew the Japanese army towards a magnificent mountain in Hubei province, and this ruse spared the rest of their battalion. Then, preferring to die rather than surrender, they threw themselves off the mountain after destroying their weapons, crying: 'Down with Japanese imperialism, long live the Chinese Communist Party!' Three of the men died; two, Ge Zhenlin and Song Xueyi, miraculously survived, saved by tree branches. Their heroism has been celebrated by the regime ever since and even features in schoolbooks.

Two years before the grand parade in Beijing, the official version of this story had been questioned by a historian. The legal troubles he experienced after expressing these reservations about its authenticity are symptomatic of the regime's fight against 'historical nihilism', serving as a warning: reassessing the veracity of historical narratives is to be discouraged. The controversy started in the autumn of 2013, when the historian Hong Zhenkuai published two articles: one in the economics magazine *Caijing*, the other in the journal *Yanhuang Chunqiu* (China Through the Ages), the last bastion of the now-marginalised Party reformers. Hong underlined the 'inconsistencies and contradictions' in the Mount Langya narrative, based on testimonies and archival research. He decided to publish his findings following the arrest in August 2013 of an online poster in Canton accused of spreading 'rumours', when in fact all he had done was question the truthfulness of the 'myth'. He was sentenced to one week of administrative detention.

But the story was far from over. Not satisfied with doing right by this 'gossip', Hong naively believed that he could sue for libel the two neo-Maoist—and so pro-Xi—figures who had insulted him on social media following the online publication of his articles. But he was not the only who felt insulted. The descendants of the 'heroes' also got involved, and they in turn condemned both the historian and his editor, Huang Zhong. At the end of the first trial, Hong, having dared question this glorious example of Chinese resistance, was convicted. In a lengthy text published in October 2016, the Supreme Court would refer back to these trials, citing them as 'model cases regarding the protection of dignity of heroic figures'. In Xi's China, no-one can criticise great men. For, the judges believed, 'the Anti-Japanese War was an important component of the movement that allowed the Communist Party of China to lead the Chinese people, to overturn imperialist domination, and to arrive at a new democratic revolution', and the fact that 'the Communist Party of China had played a central role in the Anti-Japanese War has become the consensus of the whole nation.' What is more, the judges declared,

> The 'Heroes of Mount Langya', as figureheads for heroic deeds and people, have become models of the Chinese nation's bravery and sacrifice ... Any inappropriate comment and judgement of such heroic figures and their actions hurt the public's national sentiments, and trigger public criticism, and even provoke emotional reactions.

Hong and his editor, then, should have anticipated the ferocious criticism and negative rulings that would arise from their thesis, and 'should have shown a higher degree of tolerance.' In short, they only got what they deserved after seeking to undermine the official historical narrative. But their troubles were still not behind them.

In a second court case, the author and editor were sued by the children of the two survivors. This time the judges went further; in attacking these soldiers, it was the country's very honour that had been assaulted:

> In this time of peace, the spirit of the heroes of Mount Langya permanently guide us in the struggle for the people and the country to be fearless in the face of challenges and difficulties ... And seen from a legal or a historical perspective, the collective memories of the nation are an integral part of the public interest. Therefore, the articles that Hong Zhenkuai wrote have not only harmed the reputations and honour of Ge Zhenlin and Song Xueyi, but also the public interest.

Thus, without so much as a glance at the historian's evidence, the judges ordered him to issue a public apology to the heroes' descendants, which he declined to do. To quote the protagonist of George Orwell's *1984*, Ministry of Truth employee Winston Smith, 'Who controls the present controls the past'.

Since this case, a similar punishment has befallen a blogger who had dared mock Qiu Shaoyun, a Chinese hero of the Korean War. What is striking is how seriously the Chinese state treats these issues. The matter was even raised by several delegates during a parliamentary session, in March 2017. Following this intervention, the National People's Assembly added a new provision to the General Provisions of the Civil Law, to be enacted in 2020: it will hold people accountable for damaging the reputation and honour of Revolutionary heroes and martyrs. This is the culmination of a long-held policy. In autumn 2016, just before an important political meeting, official media had published an article entitled 'Xi Jinping: History Cannot Be Denied', looking back at a selection of speeches by the Chinese leader in which he foregrounds 'historical nihilism' as the main threat in play. He quotes the thinker Gong Zizhen (1792–1841) on this matter: 'To destroy a state, one must first erase its history.' He added, 'The hostile, foreign or interior forces that often write about the Chinese Revolution and the new China never cease to attack, slander, and tarnish: the principal objective is to confound people.'

But from where does this 'historical nihilism', so maligned by Xi Jinping, come? From the West, China's official historians reply, unblinkingly. Three of them— Yu Pei, from the Institute of World History of the Chinese Academy of Social Sciences; Zheng Zhiqu, professor at the School of History of Beijing Normal University; and Yang Jun, professor at the School of Marxism of Wuhan University—outlined this theory in great detail in a full-page *People's Daily* article of 20 February 2017.

According to Yang Jun, 'postmodernism' came to dominate Western intellectual circles in the mid-twentieth century, 'as the West entered a post-industrial era'. The primary objective of the accompanying new historiography was to deconstruct and to 'destroy' traditional historiography. Its aim, Yang argued, was to oppose the 'great narrative' that it accused of supporting Marxist material history: this new historiography 'denies the "continuity" of history and deliberately seeks to "tear it to pieces", it questions and subverts its scientific and objective character, denying the existence of objective reality; it dissolves history into a pure literary imaginary; it believes that the latter is nothing but a type of narrative.' This is the source of 'historical nihilism'. 'It appeared here for complex international and national reasons,' Yang continued:

On an international level, due to technological and technical development and the growth of globalisation, capitalism showed a definite vitality and force with which to control the world, whilst the development of socialism encountered difficulties due to turmoil in the Soviet Union. This posed theoretical challenges to Marxist historical materialism. At the domestic level, policies of reform and opening up led to deep-felt changes in the economic and social structure of our country, social values became more diversified and some schools of thought in favour of Westernisation developed. And this fostered the growth of 'historical nihilism'. Obviously, in history departments, some academics followed the lead of Western historical research and theories, which they supposedly developed, but in fact purely and simply imitated. In terms of academic methodology, their approach is very unilateral, and lacks dialectic thought.

On the next page, Zheng Zhiqu blamed a series of intellectual currents linked to Western contemporary thinkers: 'Jacques Derrida's deconstructionism', 'Martin Heidegger's existentialism', 'Hayden White's meta-history', 'Jean-François Lyotard's anti-grand narrative'. All sought, in his eyes, to 'eliminate at all costs historical tradition and objectivity'. They had erased in one stroke 'the theory, the principles and the methods of rational historiography'. He further lamented postmodernism's still-significant influence in China, given that it had started to decline 'in international academia in the 1990s'.

These are academics who go to great lengths to present historical nihilism as a consequence of an intellectual fad, imported from the West, which is both foreign and even hostile to historical materialism. Their works can only please the regime. To suggest that criticism of Chinese history might be a perverse effect of postmodernism is a very clever trick indeed.

Xi Jinping can only rejoice at this sophisticated theorisation by intellectuals. It serves his purpose, which is to obtain absolute control over the writing of history. More than any other leader since Mao, he has understood that controlling the past is vital. He intends to twist it in the direction desired by the Party, and this is one of his great projects. This is all the more noticeable when contrasted with the (very) relative free speech that had been characteristic of the 2000s, which disappeared almost from one day to the next. At that time, historians or journalists dared write about topics such as the Great Leap Forward, the accelerated movement of industrial modernisation driven forward by the Great Helmsman, which lead to millions of deaths in rural areas; or the Hundred Flowers Campaign and the Anti-Rightist Campaign of 1957. But under Xi Jinping's mandate, there has been a return to pure historical orthodoxy—and to the most hackneyed forms of control.

Thus, in February 2016, the former *Xinhua* journalist Yang Jisheng was denied permission to travel to the United States, where he was to be awarded a prize. Author of a book published in Hong Kong (and banned in China) on the Great Famine of 1958–62, which resulted from the failure of the Great Leap Forward, Yang had estimated the number of dead at 36 million. Harvard University wanted to reward him in the name of 'conscience and integrity in journalism'. Unable to travel to receive the award, he sent the speech he had planned to give, its words a resounding condemnation of the new obscurantism imposed by Xi:

> We must remember not only the good things, but also the bad; not only the brightness, but also the darkness. ... My book *Tombstone* recorded a horrific man-made disaster that lasted for several years. Although it could only be published in Hong Kong and remains banned in China, truth-loving people have found various means and channels to distribute it throughout mainland China. ... Fact is a powerful bomb that blasts lies to smithereens. Fact is a beacon in the night that lights the road of progress. Fact is the touchstone of truth; there can be no truth without facts.

In another tightening of the screw, 2016 saw the take-over of *Yanhuang Chunqiu* (China Through the Ages), the journal founded in the 1990s by a group of retired officials. It had been the bastion of the Party's reformist wing, whose members included Hu Yaobang and Zhao Ziyang. The death of the former in 1989 had led to the democratic marches and events at Tiananmen; Zhao had been put under house arrest following the bloody repression of these protests. The journal's editorial board was replaced in summer 2016 by members of the Neo-

Maoist movement—the same individuals, in fact, who had insulted the historian Hong Zhenkuai. One of them, Guo Songmin, celebrated this victory by posting a quote from one of Mao's poems on Weibo (Chinese social media): 'Today the autumn wind still sighs,/But the world has changed!' One of the deposed journal editors commented: 'These are people who wish to cover up the dark side of history.'

Controlling history involves promoting a founding myth. In France it's the Revolution, in Britain its *Magna Carta*. Xi Jinping celebrates the Long March (1934–6), the epic journey of the Red Army. Mao became leader of the Party at the Zunyi Conference of January 1935, during this trek across China—12,000 kilometres from south to north—which had started off as a flight from the Nationalist forces. From its northern retreat, in 'Yellow Earth' China, the Red Army started reconquering the country. This was the beginning of the Communists' rise to power, culminating in a final victory fourteen years later.

The eightieth anniversary of the end of the Long March, celebrated in the autumn of 2016, presented Xi with the perfect opportunity to restage this mythical narrative for twenty-first-century China, making it an element of the great revival of the Chinese nation. 'This revolutionary exploit which shook the world is an incredible epic of the Communist Party and the Red Army, a stately monument in the history of the great

rejuvenation of the Chinese nation,' he declared following his visit to an exhibition on the historical event in
Beijing. China must rediscover the spirit of this 'epic,
human miracle', Xi said, once again betraying an echo of
the origins that obsess him.

> The Long March was an admirable military expedition
> for its ideas and convictions. It represents a sublime
> ideal, a firm conviction, an eternal political spirit of the
> Chinese Communist Party. Since its foundation, the
> Party has used communism to create a noble ideal and,
> from the start, to lead the Chinese people in unison
> towards that admirable ideal. The Party and the Red
> Army experienced setbacks, but persevered.

This reference to setbacks was no coincidence, for
with it Xi underlined that the Communists were ultimately victorious and overcame these setbacks through
the strength of their vision. This is a lesson for the complicated times awaiting China, as it is widely known that
its economic model—dependent on the exploitation of
natural resources and human labour—is running out of
steam. 'The suffering, difficulties and deaths on the Long
March challenged the convictions and ideals of Communist Party members, but they showed the people that
these convictions and ideals were indestructible.'

As the political scientist Raoul Girardet pointed out,
it is in moments of crisis or mutation that mythological
effervescence is at its strongest. China, under Xi Jinping,
has entered a new phase of its history, after around sixty

years that can be divided into two distinct periods: thirty years of Maoism, and thirty years of 'socialist market economy'. Xi hopes that the Long March will become the new myth of the present:

> The Red Army's victorious march amply reflects the great force and spirit of the revolutionary ideal. Times and circumstances have changed, but for us members of the Communist Party, the ideals and causes we fight for have not changed. You should commit to memory the glorious exploits of the Red Army, promote its spirit, develop and spread traditional revolutionary and patriotic education.

This is why the Soviet Union is a counter-example in Xi's eyes, for the Soviet leaders sowed the seeds of their own downfall in giving up on the ideological struggle. Yet the fact remains that it is uncertain whether a mythology can be decreed from on high.

As we have seen, some commentators had seen in Xi Jinping a potential reformer. It was thought that if he followed in Deng's footsteps he would be capable of facing serenely the Party's past, whether the horrors of Maoism or the repression of the Tiananmen movement in 1989. These predictions were based on Xi's personal history: had not his own father been the victim of one of Mao's purges in 1962? Had he not himself been sent to the countryside along with millions of other youths during the Cultural Revolution?

But, just as with hopes of political reform, so it was with hopes of historical revisionism: disillusion came swiftly. No later than 5 January 2013, the newly anointed Xi presented his vision before the new full and alternate members of the Central Committee, at the Central Party School in Beijing. The history of the Party was a whole, he said, and it was impossible to fragment it or to retain one part but not another. This was a fundamental warning, articulated by the regime's propaganda machine in the phrase 'the two things that cannot be negated' (*liangge buneng fouding*). It is important to outline what this actually means.

Like a set designer laying the groundwork for a play to be performed, Xi began this speech by outlining a fresco of six historical eras, as the theoretical backdrop to his own interpretation. He identified the utopian socialism of the nineteenth century; Marx and Engels' devising of 'Scientific Marxism'; Lenin's October Revolution and the 'implementation of socialism'; the 'development of a scientific model'; the 'exploration and the implementation of "Socialism by the Chinese Communist Party" after the foundation of the New China'; and, finally, 'our Party's strategic decision to conduct policies of reform and opening-up and to initiate "Socialism with Chinese characteristics"'.

Xi focused more extensively on the latter two eras. For him, the thirty years of Maoism, from 1949 to 1979, and the three 'never-had-it-so-good' decades of reforms complement each other; they cannot be used against each other. In political terms, this meant that Xi struck a blow to both the left and the right. With the rise of inequality resulting from the country's strong growth, a section of the Chinese population is nostalgic for what they see as a golden age: Maoism. From this view of history Xi drew a critique of 'capitalism', which he argued had burrowed itself into the heart of the system like a worm into an apple—this is the anti-neoliberal discourse of those academics whom some call the 'New Left'. At the other end of the spectrum, the 'reformers' have for the most part dreamed of a 'de-Maoisation' similar to the de-Stalinisation that took place in the USSR in the late 1950s. They had hoped, in vain, that the regime would be more virulently critical of the Great Helmsman.

Before Xi, stock had been taken in a 1981 text, 'Resolution on Certain Questions in the History of Our Party Since the Founding of the People's Republic of China', and adopted at the Sixth Plenary Session of the Party's Eleventh Central Committee. The Party had distinguished Mao the man, guilty of the 'grave blunder of the Cultural Revolution', from 'Mao Zedong Thought', which had allowed China to become a socialist country defined by 'Marxism-Leninism applied and developed in China'. Here is the central tenet of the Resolution:

> It is entirely wrong to try to negate the scientific value of Mao Zedong Thought and to deny its guiding role in our revolution ... just because Comrade Mao Zedong made mistakes in his later years. And it is likewise entirely wrong to adopt a dogmatic attitude towards the sayings

of Comrade Mao Zedong, to regard whatever he said as the immutable truth which must be mechanically applied everywhere, and to be unwilling to admit honestly that he made mistakes in his later years, and even try to stick to them in our new activities. Both these attitudes fail to make a distinction between Mao Zedong Thought—a scientific theory formed and tested over a long period of time—and the mistakes Comrade Mao Zedong made in his later years. And it is absolutely necessary that this distinction should be made.

It is also absolutely forbidden, therefore, to use one past to spite the other; to invoke Mao against opening up, or to criticise Mao in the name of opening up.

Xi follows this tradition almost to the letter, and has taken it even further. From this perspective, his speeches show a distinct evolution from the position of the 1980s. While his predecessors were slightly embarrassed when rendering homage to Mao, Xi embraces it. He calls for a synthesis of the two first eras of the regime, the Mao era and the post-Mao era—between the Revolution, and 'Socialism with Chinese characteristics'. He wants to perpetuate a form of capitalism that is under the aegis of the Party, as imagined by Deng Xiaoping—even if this involves glossing over the Party's blunders under the rule of 'Comrade Mao'.

Our party has guided the people to build socialism during two eras, before and after the period of reform and opening up. These two eras are mutually connected even though they differ in many ways, but they were both ultimately periods when the construction of socialism was implemented and explored by our Party at the head of the people. 'Socialism with Chinese characteristics' was initiated in the new historical period of reform and opening up, but it was also initiated on the foundation of the basic socialist system already set up by the New China and on which more than twenty years of construction had taken place. Even if there are vast differences between the two in terms of ideology, governing policy and practical work, they cannot be separated, let alone be opposed to each other. The period of history that preceded opening up and the reforms cannot be negated by that which followed; nor can the period of history that preceded opening up and the reforms be used to negate the period of history after opening up and the reforms. The ideological line must be maintained: to seek truth from facts [one of the main tenets of Maoism], to distinguish between what is fundamental and what is accessory, to persevere in the truth, to revise mistakes, to have many experiences, to learn lessons; and it is from these foundations that we must continue to move forward.

With this perfectly measured early speech, Xi pulled off a brilliant balancing act. Above all, he sent a strong message: he would not make the same mistakes as had the comrades in the Soviet Union; China would on no account be 'de-Maoised'. Even better, Xi intended to retrace the path followed by his predecessors, and 're-Maoise' the regime.

This 're-Maoisation' is a superficial one—it is not about returning to collectivism and the permanent revolution that destabilised society under Mao—but it has nevertheless been spectacular. The man of the hour is cited in every speech once more. Xi probably sees this loyalty as a necessity. The regime may constantly assert that it is the product of 'a civilisation with 5,000 years of uninterrupted history', but it is relatively young in its current, communist form: only seventy years old. Like all new countries, socialist China must create a genealogy for itself. Mao is unavoidable—he is at once Lenin and Stalin, both the founder and the dictator wrapped up in one man; a leader who overthrew one order and established another. To tear him down would risk the collapse of the whole system. To weaken him is to weaken the country; of this Xi appears convinced.

The 120th anniversary of Mao's birth in December 2013 gave Xi the opportunity to present his vision of the great man. While making some concessions to the spirit of the 1981 text—'Mao made grave mistakes'—he praised his glorious predecessor highly. To hear Xi, Mao was not only China's half-mummified founding father, commemorated at the beginning of every speech, but also a living figure, invoked when looking to the future. Far from being a fossil, a mere ghost, he represents promise. Xi minimised Mao's mistakes and insisted at length on his genius. Of course he made mistakes, for 'revolutionary leaders are not gods, but human beings':

Even if they possess a high degree of theoretical thought, rich experience of conflict and extraordinary leadership skills, that does not mean that their knowledge and their actions were not limited by conditions at the time ... we cannot totally repudiate them and erase their historical feats just because they made mistakes.

In other words, situations need to be put back into their historical and social contexts—and Mao's guilt minimised. 'Comrade Mao Zedong's mistakes in his later years have their subjective factors and a portion of personal responsibility, but complicated social and historical reasons both at home and abroad also played their part. They should be viewed and analysed comprehensively, historically and dialectically.'

For Xi, what was essential was that Mao devised a unique philosophy, 'Mao Zedong Thought'. From this early speech in his leadership, from its flight of lyricism tinged with communist jargon, we understand what it meant to Xi Jinping to respect 'the living soul of Mao Zedong Thought'. This soul could be found in the three main principles he wished to follow in governing the country: first 'seeking truth from facts' (pragmatism), then the 'mass line', then 'independence'. This trinity of tools had become empty shells; its return has been deliberate, and no one has breathed new life into it like Xi has. This is how the Chinese leader distinguishes himself from his predecessors: he appears truly to seek his path through an in-depth reinterpretation of Maoist dogma.

It would be mistaken to believe that his many homages to the Great Helmsman are a mere show of formal esteem, the paying of lip-service. Upon close examination, Xi's speeches suggest that he sincerely believes Mao's political legacy to be perfectly relevant today.

5

THE HEROIC FATHER

Xi Jinping's historical universe is populated by heroes. Those praised by the regime since 1949: all the men and women who took part in the Long March and fought for the rise of communism. The cult of Red heroes is comparable to that of saints. They are celebrated, acclaimed; their exemplary lives are the subject of hagiographic texts. Xi's generation was the first to have grown up listening to these glorious stories. And he can personally double his claim to such adulation, for his own father, Xi Zhongxun, had been one of those heroes, one of Mao's companions. Enrolled as a teenager into the guerrillas based in the north-east, he had joined the Revolution's avant-garde.

Contrary to widespread perceptions, China did not shed its ideological skin after Mao's death. The heroic martyr narrative, as relayed by the propaganda machine, still deeply permeates the national imaginary. Xi Jinping is particularly loyal to it, and rarely misses an opportunity to revive characters from great Revolutionary myths. In a speech to Party members at the Great Hall of the People in July 2016, he embarked on a lyrical recounting of the blood spilled by the first fighters:

> History has told us that the path taken by China, the Chinese people, and the Chinese nation over the past 95 years has been paved with the blood, sweat, and tears of the Communist Party of China and the Chinese people. Full of hardship and glory, setback and victory, and sacrifice and gain, this is a splendid chapter in the history of the Chinese nation that must never be forgotten or denied ... We must always remember the unfulfilled wishes of those martyrs, and we must never forget the ideals for which they spilled their blood.

In May 2014, Xi had made the same point by striking a more personal note during a discussion in a Beijing school, when he seemed to recall happy memories of his communist childhood. Xi himself had dreamt in Technicolour of the grandiose and majestic Maoist adventure; and the young generations under his leadership would do the same. His words were almost touching:

> Children need to learn from the heroes and avant-garde personalities and keep a positive attitude throughout their studies. There are many young heroes in our history, and in the revolution, the construction and reform that were brought about by the people under the Party's leadership. You must have learned the names of some of them through films such as *Red Children, Little Soldier*

Zhang Ka, Feather Letter, The Little Heroic Soldier and
Heroic Little Sisters from the Grassland.

This speech brought together history and myth. There
was no difference between reality and the legends portrayed on screen; teaching must foster communist fervour in today's youth—and under no circumstances a
critical mind.

Xi's speeches, then, are filled with references to this
propaganda-constructed imaginary. Having faded somewhat during the Deng Xiaoping years, it has now been
restored to its former glory. As in the Soviet Union,
since its founding in 1949 Communist China has always
celebrated the figure of the hero-martyr, whether
worker, soldier, or peasant. The hero-martyr appears in
literature, cinema, and the pages of *The People's Daily*,
the Party's official newspaper. Even though educating
the masses is not unique to the People's Republic of
China, the young Republic was particularly militant in
doing so. In an article written in 1969, during the
Cultural Revolution, the French legal expert Philippe
Ardant pointed out that about forty new such figures
had appeared between 1963 and 1968. The hero-making
factory was incredibly productive:

> The organisation of these campaigns was remarkable. In
> the space of a few weeks, a previously unknown name
> would become familiar to the entire Chinese people.
> Someone entered their lives, influenced their behav-
> iour, reigned over their public and private acts. The use

of all the advertising techniques that had proven their worth in Western 'consumer societies' was reinforced by the authorities' grip, and capacity to impose control, over the masses. Pointing out a subject to be studied, implied setting in motion thousands of Party cells and all the organisations that envelop the professional and private lives of individuals.

One of China's new 'saints', who rose and was ranked from the 1960s onwards alongside virtuous figures from the Confucian universe, was Lei Feng. He was a soldier born in a poor peasant family, whose story was popularised in the 1960s. According to the official narrative, he had had a terrible childhood: his father had been killed by Japanese soldiers and his mother committed suicide after she was raped by a landowner. The young orphan had been brought up by the Party. He was known for his famous sayings, such as 'When I think of the present, my heart is overwhelmed with gratitude to the Party and Chairman Mao', and, especially, 'In the great revolutionary undertaking ... I want to be a screw that will never rust'. He was a paragon of loyalty and devotion: 'A water drop dries up if it does not join the immense ocean; a man is powerless if he does not join the community.' But destiny was against him—he died in a truck accident in 1962, aged twenty-two. A year later, he was celebrated by Mao himself. We must 'study Lei Feng', declared the Great Helmsman. The worship of Lei Feng lasted throughout the Cultural Revolution and well beyond the Mao era.

It is uncertain whether Lei Feng really existed. He is nevertheless praised by the regime as a model of virtue and altruism. Schoolchildren affectionately call him 'Uncle Lei Feng'. They learn the song: 'Learn from Lei Feng, a good example, loyal to the revolution, loyal to the Party'. Every 5 March—the day in 1963 when Mao wrote the calligraphy 'Learn from Lei Feng'—the young hero is celebrated with a 'day of good deeds'. In this era of 'wild capitalism', the regime needs him now more than ever. Xi mentioned him in March 2014 when addressing an audience of soldiers during the annual session of the National People's Assembly: 'The spirit of Lei Feng is eternal, he is a living embodiment of socialist values. You must be like seeds sown in the Nation's earth to spread the spirit of Lei Feng.'

Mindful of the memory of such lives, given up for the Party and the creation of a new world, Xi made sure, shortly after becoming president in 2013, to proclaim two new 'patriotic' national holidays. 30 September became Martyr Day—to commemorate the start of construction in 1949 on a monument to the people's heroes at Tiananmen Square; 13 December commemorated the victims of the 1937 Nanking Massacre, in which, according to the Chinese authorities, 300,000 people were killed by Japanese troops in what was then the temporary capital of the Republic of China.

The heavy emphasis placed on these victims sets Xi Jinping's policies in the purest of Maoist methods. As soon as he came to power, Mao established the celebration of the spirit of sacrifice and ordered that 'narratives recalling the bitterness of the past and the happiness of the present' (*yikusitian*) be disseminated, as well as testimonies of the deeds of both 'diabolic people' (*guizi*) — the Japanese 'devils', landowners, capitalists and so on—and 'good people', the Communists. The aim of these frequently simplistic narratives was to keep alive the memory of past suffering, in order to rejoice over the better life now offered by the Party. They recalled the struggle and sacrifices that allowed new generations to live life to the fullest. Secondary school and university students, including the future Red Guards, were sent to the countryside to listen to the stories of peasants, who had in the past been oppressed by landowners, but were now deemed masters of their fate. During the Cultural Revolution (1966–76), which would allow the younger generations to re-enact the Revolutionary deeds of their elders, this Manichean world reached new heights.

In twenty-first-century China, under Xi Jinping's mandate, these narratives are back—this time, on television. Thus, at peak viewing time—early evening—on 26 October 2016, for the ninety-fifth anniversary of the Party, China's top public channel, CCTV-1, broadcast a show called *Bangyang* (model, example). 'Exemplary' members of the Party paraded on set. They represented society in all its variety: a schoolteacher from the countryside, sailors, local officials, a worker, a policewoman, a scientist. Also present were the daughter of a revolutionary martyr who talked about the Japanese 'devils', and a 104-year-old veteran of the Long March who exclaimed: 'Eighty years later, I have to recognise that the Chinese Communist Party is a glorious and just party.' 'With his memories of the Long March,' the presenter exclaimed to applause, 'a veteran reminds us of a time when people fought for their ideals. After so many years, this man's commitment has not weakened.'

Laughter featured, but so did tears. Those of a schoolteacher who sacrificed her family life to go and teach in an underprivileged mountain region, and whose daughter says in front of the camera: 'Mum, you are a good teacher, but you are not a good mother.' The tears of a policewoman whose father was also a police officer—she hated her father's job, because he spent no time with her, until he was involved in a serious accident and she realised how many people worried over him. Touched, she had then decided to join the police force herself: 'When I became a policewoman, I understood that it was not that my father did not love me or did not want to take care of me, but that he in fact had a lot of responsibilities.' As the presenter had warned the audience at the start of the show, 'An admirable era calls for an admirable spirit, noble work needs exemplary guides.'

Xi Jinping has a particular fondness for those Party officials who have been models of respectability. He invokes their memory above all others'. Among those in his personal hall of fame is Jiao Yulu, a typical example of the honest dignitary. He worked himself into an early grave, pursuing his work despite his liver cancer worsening day by day. Jiao died in 1964, and became the object of a campaign of national celebration launched by Mao Zedong two years later, at the start of the Cultural Revolution. The Party needed a figure to rally behind, for it was on the verge of collapse. According to his official biography, in 1966, when Xi was still in middle school, he had been moved by a professor unable to suppress his sobs as he read out a *People's Daily* article on Jiao Yulu. A few years later, in 1990, when he was a young, early-career official, Xi dedicated a short poem to Jiao Yulu: 'Who, among the people, cannot but love as good an official as Jiao Yulu! ... neither snow at night nor morning frost can cool a hero's zeal.'

Today, Jiao has proven very useful to the anticorruption campaign. In March 2014, Xi travelled with the entirety of the Politburo Standing Committee to Lankao county, Henan province, where a memorial to the model official had been erected. This trip can be understood within the framework of the current 'mass line' campaign. Jiao personified this Maoist concept that is so important, even seminal, to the Xi regime: officials must mingle with the people, throw themselves among them, learn from them, as well as guide them. Xi is revamping this dialectic, which was dear to Mao's heart. At the site of the memorial, he said:

Jiao Yulu is a model for county-level Party secretaries [one of the lowest echelons in the Chinese administration], and he is also a model for the whole Party. Even if he left us fifty years ago, people continue to praise his actions, his spirit can be associated with the spirit of the Jinggang Mountains [a range in central China where Mao assembled his forces after 1927], of Yan'an, of Lei Feng. All belong to the revolutionary tradition of yesterday, of today and of tomorrow. It is a precious spiritual resource for our party, we must always learn from it.

In September 2015, Xi sang Jiao's praises once more in a meeting with local officials training at the Central Party School. He invoked a 'Jiao Yulu style' to which all those wishing to become 'Communist Party County Committee Secretaries' must adhere. One must always have 'in mind the Party, the people, a sense of responsibility', and always 'be vigilant'. 'If the style of the County Committee Secretary leaves something to be desired, then the image the masses will have of the Party will deteriorate,' he warned.

Indeed, one year later, a scandal underlined the magnitude of this task. An official of a rural town in Hebei province was caught on camera dining in an upscale lobster restaurant. In the video, disseminated on social media, the man—who is quite plump—shares his thoughts on the masses: 'Their bowls are full of rice, their mouths full of pork, but when they have finished eating they criticise the government. The Chinese masses are shameless and are not worthy of our respect.' The troublemaker was removed from his position, of course. But his words doubtless reflected what other officials think of their constituents—a far cry from the wonderful propaganda slogans.

A news item in February 2015 showed the extent of resentment towards local officials. Jia Jinglong, a young resident of a village near Shijiazhuang, Hebei province, killed the mayor using a modified nail gun. It was an act of vengeance against the official who, two years previously, had ordered the destruction of the family home into which the newly-wed Jia was to move. He had not got any compensation following the house's demolition, and his fiancée later left him. He was sentenced to death and executed in November 2016, but his case led to the mobilisation of several legal experts, as well as attracting the support of the blogosphere and some of the press, who were moved by this miscarriage of justice.

No wonder, then, that Xi Jinping emphasised the seriousness of even junior offices in a meeting with local officials in September 2015. Xi, who had been Party branch secretary in a village in Shaanxi before embarking on the career that would lead him to the highest echelons of power, stressed that 'it is not a very senior position, but the responsibilities and the pressure are no less important. It is difficult to have such responsibility.' He then referred to another model official: Gu Wenchang, who died in 1981 at the age of thirty-four, and who had fought all his life against desertification—one of the main environmental challenges facing northern China, where water resources are low.

Gu Wenchang's profile of selfless devotion to the people is similar to Jiao Yulu's. Xi used his example to sing the praises of the lower-level cadre, an essential link in the Chinese administrative chain of command:

> In the Party's organisation and the political structure of the country, the lower-level cadre stands at a crucial level between the top and the bottom. This is fundamental to economic development, ensuring the people's well-being, and keeping and promoting the peace. The elders said that if the prefectures and counties are well governed, then the country will be at peace. Our country's county system dates back to the "Spring and Autumn period", and since the Qin dynasty promoted it, it has become stronger and more developed. For two thousand years, the county has been an elementary unit of our national structure and endures to this day. Different imperial dynasties have always attached great importance to lower-level officials for selection and for promotion. The elders summarised it as follows: the prime minister comes from the prefecture, worthy soldiers from the troops. There are many famous leaders in our history who came from the counties.

The similarity between the two local officials praised by Xi lay not only in their frugality, but also in their proximity to the masses, which the leader described as an ancestral virtue dating back to the ancient dynasties.

Both represent the 'good side' of the Party, as opposed to its dark side, rife with scheming and concubines. 'Micro-corruption [of lower-level officials] can grow into a great disaster,' the Chinese leader warned in January 2016, during the sixth plenum of the Central Commission for Discipline Inspection, the government body in charge of anti-corruption and order.

So far as we can see, counter-models are equally important in Xi's descriptions of society. Repulsive figures—officials who succumb to bribery, easy money, nepotism—are singled out in his speeches, exposed in all their excesses and their villainy. 'Many Party officials have lost touch with the people,' he warned in the same 2016 speech, 'and some problems are very serious, particularly the "four vices" of formalism, bureaucracy, hedonism and extravagance.'

'Formalism', in communist terminology, means letting things go for the sake of appearance, neglecting efficiency, and hiding behind paperwork. This accusation is aimed at those who have not studied Party theory seriously, contenting themselves with a cursory knowledge of it. 'They do not intend to educate themselves, nor do they have the ability to seriously put their knowledge into practice'. The speech also targeted those who had fallen into the habit of calling for the preparation of documents and convening meetings, simply to generate more documents and more meetings. Such formalists, Xi continued, also enjoy showing off. 'Their sole objective is to ingratiate themselves with their superiors, to make the front page or to gild their work reports, one ceremony after another, one report after another, one prize after another.' He likened bureaucrats in this vein to the pompous journalist Krikun in Oleksandr Korniychuk's play *The Front*.

As for bureaucracy, in the Chinese communist sense it can be defined as losing all concept of reality and losing touch with the population: 'Some do not know the real situation and do not want to give it any heed. They do not want to visit difficult regions, nor help baseline organisations and the people solve their problems. They prefer to not meet them and avoid complications. Their work is a game.' Hedonism, meanwhile, is characterised by 'the weakening of spirit, inertia, the quest for honours and riches, the desire for wellbeing, for comfort, for pomp and for pleasure'. Certain Party officials are 'demoralised, and their convictions have been shattered'. At the same time, 'their life philosophy is "drink while there is wine" and "take every opportunity to have fun and make the most of it"'. Extravagance, the last of the four sins, constitutes 'waste, excessive spending, major construction projects, multiple parties and festivals, and a luxurious, self-indulgent and idle lifestyle, abuses of power for personal gain and corruption.' Xi went on to describe these offences in detail:

> Some Party officials spend hundreds of millions of yuan to build sumptuous buildings for their offices that

measure no less than 100 *mu* (7 hectares), that are decorated like palaces, and have leisure facilities. Others indulge in organising parties and ceremonies for which they easily spend millions of yuan. What a waste of human and material resources! Others seek comfort and pleasure, spacious lodgings, luxury cars, refined dishes and clothing by major brands. Their excesses show that they flaunt the rules, take their privileges for granted, and always want more. Others demand a welcome beyond their rank, wish to stay in luxury hotels, eat all sorts of exquisite foods, drink fine wines, before asking for 'little presents'. Others have loyalty cards and high-value credit cards to have fun in night clubs and high-end sports clubs, to travel for free in China and abroad, and even to spend lavishly in casinos abroad! Finally, others glorify their antics and their moral corruption rather than feel ashamed of them.

The picture Xi paints is a haunting one, and the level of detail in his description of deviancies affecting the Party today is striking. This precision is an admittance of the state of the regime, but it also demonstrates the shrewdness of the all-seeing and all-knowing Party. Officials must fear its clear-sightedness and be wary of imminent punishment.

To illustrate even more accurately the regime's determination to eliminate these bad eggs, the Central Commission for Discipline Inspection co-produced a documentary television series. Broadcast in the autumn of 2016, at the time of the Sixth Plenum of the Eighteenth

Party Congress, and entitled *Always on the Road (Yongyuan zai lushang)*, its budget was on par with many Western journalistic productions. The series was watched at every echelon of the Party, during compulsory—or at least highly recommended—screenings. It opens with Xi Jinping's uplifting 2015 New Year wishes:

> We will continue to comprehensively strengthen party governance and discipline. We will unswervingly transform our working style, be tough on corruption ... In this socialist country led by the Communist Party of China, any corrupt official who is exposed will be dealt with. All those involved in corruption and embezzlement will be punished or prosecuted. The people put us in power, and we must devote ourselves to the Party, to the country, and protect them. We must do what we must; those who break the law must be punished. If we do not punish the hundreds of thousands of corrupted officials, it is an offence to 1.3 billion Chinese people. It is a political duty that we must always keep in mind, a debt owed to the people.

The series was a craftily-staged montage of stories of corrupt officials, mostly followed by videos of their self-criticism sessions, and the testimonies of the formidable inspectors of the dreaded Central Commission for Discipline Inspection. The eight episodes enthralled the country, for they revealed the inner workings of the Party, and the corruption that exists at every level. The episode exposed officials who were tempted by pleasure, money, power and ambition, and who put *si* (private affairs) before *gong* (public interest).

One such official was Bai Enpei, former Party secretary of the southern province of Yunnan, who had started his career in Xi's beloved Yellow Earth region, where revolutionary purity was meant to prevail. Bai Enpei doubly betrayed the Party, the documentary suggests. First, he let himself be corrupted: 'After I turned sixty, I was ill, and I started looking for money,' he confesses on camera, from prison. But, above all, he had forgotten his roots: 'I lost faith in the ideal,' he explains. 'I then lost my integrity and crossed the red line of respect for the law. I regret it, I don't know how I—a Party Provincial Committee secretary brought up for years by the Party—came to this. I caused the Party a lot of harm. I was corrupt, but I hope that the central authorities will double their efforts to fight against corruption. Since the Eighteenth Congress, they have taken a series of measures to strictly manage the Party, to seriously investigate corruption; they are the Party's beacon of hope. Only in this way can the Party carry out its historical responsibility.' Undoubtedly, this was a well-orchestrated kind of repentance.

As the series showed, Xi, 'father of morality', makes use of an old Maoist technique in his campaign for purity: self-criticism. This technique is used primarily within the Party ranks. In September 2013, Xi spent three days in Hebei province, on the outskirts of Beijing. He presided over a series of meetings of local officials, after which the Xinhua news agency reported that some made had amends: "'After we were promoted and had been officials for a long time ... we started feeling over-confident and arrogant,' a senior Hebei cadre said. "We began merely glancing at 'shop fronts' and rarely checking out 'the backyards' and 'corners' during inspection trips.'" Xi promised to 'rectify' this neglectful behaviour. 'Criticism and self-criticism are good medicine and they embody true consideration and concern for one's comrades and oneself,' he pointed out to rows of officials scrupulously taking notes. 'Conducting criticism and self-criticism requires courage and Party spirit, and we must not abandon this weapon that protects us and cures our illnesses. Sincere words may grate on one's ears, and good medicine may be bitter. However, as Communist Party members we must lay our views on the table.'

Xi also administers this sometimes-bitter medicine— another analogy borrowed from Mao—to enemies of the Party. Unmasking pernicious individuals is one of his obsessions. He does not hesitate to use extreme measures against those who harm the regime—or those opportunely deemed to be harmful—such as ordering the broadcast of televised confessions at peak times. Corrupt officials, dissidents, even foreigners convicted of pro-democratic activities—nowadays, few escape these public acts of contrition, which had ceased after the Cultural Revolution. In August 2013, the first victims were a

Chinese-American entrepreneur, Xue Manzi, who had posted criticisms of the regime on his Weibo account, which had 12 million followers. Arrested for sleeping with a prostitute—some say it was only a pretext—he publicly apologised, and expressed his regret at having 'hurt the Chinese People': 'I committed a crime ... I hope the government will give me the opportunity to turn over a new leaf and start a new life. I recognise my mistakes. I won't do it again.'

Foreigners can also be victims of these methods, as was the case of the Swede Peter Dahlin in January 2016. Found guilty of supporting human rights lawyers, he related the ordeal a year later to *The Guardian*. He was interrogated for twenty-three days in a secret prison near Beijing and deprived of sleep. He had agreed to a televised confession knowing it would speed up his liberation. He was given A4 pieces of paper on which were printed the replies to questions from CCTV journalists: 'I have been given good food, plenty of sleep and I have suffered no mistreatments of any kind. I have no complaints to make. I think my treatment has been fair'; 'I violated Chinese law through my activities here. I have caused harm to the Chinese government. I have hurt the feelings of the Chinese people. I apologise sincerely for this and I am very sorry that this has happened'.

In 2015, Bi Fujian, a famous Chinese television presenter, was also forced to apologise and engage in self-criticism for crimes of lese-majesty against Mao. His particular crime? During a dinner party, he had sung a parody of a passage from a Revolutionary opera that was in vogue during the Cultural Revolution. He was caught on camera. In the video, he can be seen entertaining his audience by calling Chairman Mao a 'son of a bitch', or by crying out: 'He has hurt us'. This send-up of an aria from *Taking Tiger Mountain by Strategy* went viral. Needless to say, the authorities were not amused; nor was Bi's employer, the powerful central television station which broadcasts countless channels and is both the voice of the government and one of the pillars of Party propaganda. That one of its stars should target the founder of Communist China was enough to provoke a national scandal. The presenter was first promised a 'strict punishment' before being dismissed. Contrite, he posted a short message on his Weibo account: 'My comments have had a grave and undesirable impact on society, and I feel at once guilty and distressed. I apologise sincerely to everyone.'

Another victim of these confessions, Peter Humphrey, a British private investigator accused by the Chinese authorities in 2013 of obtaining illegal information, was detained for two years. He believes this practice has roots in ancient history: 'We cannot blame the party alone', he wrote in 2016.

> This situation has roots going back 2,000 years. Prevailing attitudes to the law can be traced to China's unifier and first emperor, Qin Shi Huang, who gov-

erned with no right of defence, and disregarded Confucian emphasis on rule by morality. This ideological conflict has permeated Chinese history. The deficit in rule of law is at the root of the Party's conflicts with society and of China's conflicts with the world. A major improvement would be to disconnect the justice system from the party, give judges independence to adjudicate and lawyers freedom to advocate. The country is mired in age-old practice, where the law is a toy owned and bent by the powerful. Until that changes, nobody in China will be safe.

Xi Jinping sees things very differently. His personal conviction is that, in order not to lose itself, China needs to return to the zeal of the early days, and to avoid moving towards an independent judiciary system, a hallmark of Western democracy. This return to roots, mocked at times by some of the population, involves a revival of great Party myths. The USSR had made a mistake in allowing Stalin to fall from grace after his death. In rehabilitating Mao, Xi is resolutely doing the opposite.

6

BACK TO THE CLASSICS

Xi Jinping likes to write and show off the extent of his literary knowledge. Since starting out in the Party bureaucracy in the 1980s, he has frequently written for local newspapers, without, however, claiming to be a 'real' writer, as Mao did. Whether prose or poetry, Xi's works are always political. Between 2003 and 2007, he was Party secretary of the eastern, coastal province of Zhejiang, one of the wealthiest in the country. He regularly published a column under a pseudonym in the *Zhejiang Daily*. His pen name is Zhe Xin, its two characters meaning 'wise' and 'happy'; it is also a homophonic play, echoing both Zhejiang province and *xinxi*, meaning 'joyful'. The future leader—the 'happy philosopher', 'the joyous sage'—had many plans in store.

While he writes in an overblown style typical of officials educated in the Party schools, Xi has always been keen to include quotations from classical authors in his texts. Apart from Hu's prime minister Wen Jiabao

(2003–13), Xi is the first Chinese leader since Mao to quote the classics with such ease. His reading of great texts since primary school appears to have had a marked effect on him. He draws stylistic inspiration from his readings; does he also find in them new ways of thinking about the world around him, of meditating on power or the deeds of men?

The first observation we can make is that he does not neglect a single school of Chinese thought. This wide-ranging borrowing is above all a sign that he finds the Marxist-Leninist base solid enough to graft onto it the long history of 'wonderful Chinese civilisation'. In the twenty-first century, the Party has taken possession of the entire history of the country—of '5,000 years of continuous civilisation'. Its officials are encouraged to study this history, along with Marxist thought. 'Leadership cadres must study history and culture, especially traditional Chinese culture, to enrich their wisdom and perfect their personality through study,' Xi declared on 1 March 2013, the Central Communist Party School's eightieth anniversary. 'China's traditional culture is both extensive and profound, and to acquire the essence of various thoughts is beneficial to the formation of a correct world view, outlook on life, and sense of values'.

So what are the key sources that Xi uses, bolstered by the might of his impressive propaganda machine? One important influence has been the authors of the Warring States period of the fifth to third centuries BCE. Their status in China is equivalent to that of the Ancient Greeks in the West. While it has become less common in Europe for politicians to cite the classics, it is almost second-nature in China. These authors are the fertile soil of a literary and philosophical culture shared by the educated urban populations: the Warring States period has left a lasting mark on Chinese society. It was a period of striking intellectual fertility, characterised by its great political instability: the seven states—Qi, Chu, Han, Zhao, Wei, Yan, and Qin—were constantly at war with each other. Rivalries between thinkers were more peaceful, but no less intense. At the time, scholars travelled between states, seeking employment as advisors to the rulers. On the road they would often offer their services and knowledge, which they obviously had to showcase as being the most developed and steadfast—and so the most capable of bringing strength and prestige to their prospective employers.

In the century preceding the Warring States, Confucius had tried to 'establish some principles in a world full of chaos'. He was the first to act as a moral leader or mentor, namely in terms of governance through his advice and recommendations to rulers. He was 'a master of wisdom and an uncrowned king', as Roger Darrobers elegantly puts it, and his authority was rarely questioned. His heirs, on the other hand, were faced with tough competition: it is said that there were no fewer than 100 rival schools at the time. Volume upon volume of thought remains from that era—abundant resources available to Xi Jinping today, which he does not hesitate to quote.

One of these intellectual schools is the *Tao* or *Dao*, literally the 'Way'. Taoism, which developed in the fourth and third centuries BCE, is both a school of philosophy and a 'religion of salvation' that places special emphasis on meditation and concentration: the 'aim of the adept is to achieve immortality'. Under the Tang dynasty (seventh to tenth centuries) Taoism became a semi-official state religion, and this continued during the Song dynasty (tenth to thirteenth centuries). While there is no proof that the religion's principal figure, Laozi, ever existed, there is no doubt concerning its fundamental text, known as the *Laozi* or the *Daodejing* (The Book of the Way and Virtue). Xi uses it indiscriminately and more than any other text, applying it to every context, referring to its lessons of wisdom, and quoting its proverbs.

On a trip to Berlin in March 2014, for instance, he referred to the *Daodejing* to explain his definition of soft power, pronouncing that 'a big country should be as inclusive as the lower reaches of a river, admitting numerous tributaries'. He also used it in a March 2013 interview with media from BRICS countries to explain his role as leader: 'Governing a big country is as delicate as frying a small fish'. In other words, just as stirring too much spoils the frying, the people cannot be stirred too much by frequent changes, and their interests must be taken into account.

He had used the *Daodejing* along the same lines in writing, in a 2007 collection of articles aimed at cadres, looking to persuade readers to be pragmatic rather than launching into ambitious projects. Xi quoted this adage: 'To accomplish a series of great acts through a series of small ones'. Xi has equally used the *Daodejing* to frame his foreign policy: celebrating the fiftieth anniversary of Sino-French diplomatic relations in 2014, he remarked, 'A French proverb says: "*Petit à petit, l'oiseau fait son nid* [Slow and steady wins the race]". The Chinese equivalent goes: "A towering tree grows out of a small seedling; a nine-storeyed terrace begins with heaps of earth." The Sino-French friendship is the fruit of both peoples' continued efforts.'

There have been many other such instances. To any educated Chinese person, the source of Xi's words is obvious. He is demonstrating that he too has inherited his culture from a grandiose civilisation, and that from here on in it is good to be proud of it, as the propaganda incessantly repeats. However, these signals aimed at the Chinese people are nothing more than a marketing ploy. It would be wrong to claim that Xi is a leader inspired by Taoism in his practice of power.

Xi also appears to be influenced by another major school of thought: Legalism, also known as 'realism'. Here, 'real' must be understood in the context of its use in the term 'realpolitik'. The term was coined by Han Fei, or Han Feizi, who lived from 280 to 233 BCE. Despite being influenced by Taoism, overall he believed that human nature was truly evil, and that this should be taken into account when setting up a lasting and strong government. He devised a political system based on laws benefitting the strong man and a strong country. Like Ancient Rome in the West, China was the cradle of legal thought—in the sense that law was intended to serve, and not to curb, power, let alone to separate it. As Han writes, the law includes 'rewards that are due to the careful observers of laws, and punishments that are inflicted on offenders against orders. It is what the subjects and ministers take as a model. If the ruler is tactless, delusion will come to the superior; if the subjects and ministers are lawless, disorder will appear among the inferiors. Thus, neither can be dispensed with: both are implements of emperors and kings.' Westerners, always quick to conquer and familiarise what is foreign, saw in this an indigenous version of Hobbes or Machiavelli. In any case, fear of the law is what regulates the conduct of men, according to the Legalists.

In China, Han Fei is especially known for his influence on the emperor Qin Shi Huang (259–10 BCE), who unified the country. The latter, persuaded by his philosopher-councillor, established Legalism as the official ideology of the State: 'imposing the need to rule the country through written, public, universal, and irrevocable laws.' For Stéphanie Balme, specialist in the Chinese judicial system, 'the study of the rule of law, seen as strict and punitive, was an answer at the time to a desire for the unity and stability of the empire'. Legalism indeed contributed to the establishment of a unified regime, a decisive step in the country's history, before Confucianism—whose thought on man and power is very different—imposed itself on the ruling elites.

Mao unashamedly laid claim to the revolution brought about by the Legalists. Just like the first emperor, he brought about a new, strong regime that wiped the slate clean, drawing a line under two millennia of empire. He described his own leadership as 'Marx plus Qin Shi Huang'. Xi, by contrast, does not follow in Han Fei's footsteps to the same extent. He merely cites him—a good deal. Thus, on the sixtieth anniversary of the National People's Assembly, in September 2014, Xi quoted the following phrase: 'when those who uphold the law are strong, the state is strong. When they are weak, the state is weak'. It has also often been said that Han Fei is Xi's 'favourite philosopher'. This may be an exaggeration, but it is an interesting line of enquiry. Han Fei put forward three elements: *shi* (authority), *shu* (governance)—literally the 'recipe', that is to say the techniques, with which to govern a country—and *fa*, the law that must be upheld on pain of severe punishment.

Since coming to power, Xi does indeed appear to have put these ancient teachings into practice. He has reinforced his control over the Party, the government, and the army, *shi*; deployed his 'governance' to bring rivals into line and to silence dissident voices, *shu*; all the while using the law to his advantage, *fa*. For the British sinologist Kerry Brown, Han Fei is definitely the author to look at if you want to understand Xi Jinping.

> Confucius, Mencius, Laozi and Sun Zi (of *The Art of War*) are the best known of ancient Chinese thinkers. But Han Fei deserves a wider audience. The primacy of fear, force and control to serve authority are things that linger deep in the Chinese political consciousness to this day, and have their most lucid and vivid articulation in his works. The government onslaught on even the mildest expressions of dissent and rights activism ... has puzzled many outsiders. Why does the party promote defending rule of law, and building a modern state under Xi Jinping, and yet continue to harass, imprison and abuse people like Pu Zhiqiang ...? Looking at the thinking of Han Fei gives at least some clues. In the end, it is about authority, and the need to preserve this. Authority is its own justification. It needs no excuses or explanations.

There is, however, a huge catch for any Chinese who would seriously contemplate taking Han Fei's words as the basis for modern state behaviour. The entity that he had most influence over was the Qin, which, despite its immense achievements in unifying China, collapsed under the megalomania of the founding emperor after only two decades in existence—and that emperor was a faithful follower of Han's [L]egalist school. Xi Jinping might have done more than glance at the suggestions about the exercise of power and realpolitik given in Han Fei's writings, and heed [sic] the advice about being constantly wary and on guard. But if he wants to fulfil the evidently huge ambitions he has set himself for his stewardship of his country, use of a softer, less austere thinking might be in order. At the moment, for all the talk of Confucius, Mencius and the others, it is Han Fei who seems to be winning the day.

In 2004, Qin Hui, a liberal historian and professor at Tsinghua University, caused a sensation with the release of his book *Ten Essays on Tradition*. For him, Chinese leaders had always been Confucian on the outside, while remaining Legalists in essence—in other words, proponents of governing by fear and constraint.

> What really structured traditional culture during the Imperial period was above all, under the guise of Confucian hegemony, what I would call: 'complementarity between law and Taoism' (*Fa dao hubu*). This interaction was characterised by the perpetuation of despotic power, which led to bragging and deception. Such a discretionary power could only encourage deviant behaviours and the loss of moral references, practically leaving society to the law of the jungle. In economic terms, the State intervened when the situation became chaotic, while leaving things well alone when tight control might lead to asphyxia. These two modes of action are causally linked: too much of one

leads to a change of direction that profits the other. The same type of mechanism can be found in our political culture. The need to control a world deemed chaotic and subject to the lowliest passions becomes the justification for control over society. That is the position of the Legalist. Lying to authority becomes a means of gleaning advantages and privileges from it, in other words a greater degree of 'laissez-faire' ... That is the Taoist position. This pendulum movement between Legalist and Taoist logic is a vicious circle, and the true motor of Imperial policy. That is where one must look to find the cultural origins of traditional bureaucracy's bad behaviour.

Qin Hui also unearthed the works of Tan Sitong (1865–98), a reformist scholar of the end of the Qing dynasty executed after the failure of the Hundred Days of Reform movement. For Tan, the two true schools of thought inherited from Confucianism, represented by Mencius and Zhuangzi respectively, could be termed 'democratic', for both are critiques of power. Yet, according to Tan, a philosophy influenced both by Legalism and a heterodox strain of Confucianism had prevailed by the late nineteenth century. As Qin put it, 'this now dominant movement aims to "usurp Confucius's name the better to fragment his ideals [*dao*]", and thus Confucian thought has almost completely disappeared as a result, to the benefit of unscrupulous Legalists and cynical Taoists. The latter unite their harmful effects to spread confusion.'

In many ways, China today is indeed a *yifazhiguo*, 'a country governed by law'—but in the Legalist sense of the term. It is not a 'state under the rule of law', a Western concept reviled in Xi's China, but a 'state ruled by law'— one in which the State can be totally repressive, and need not recognise the rights of individuals. Again, China is governed by a 'socialist system of laws with Chinese characteristics', as Xi explained on 4 December 2012, the thirtieth anniversary of the 1982 Constitution.

In this regard, a minor anecdote perfectly sums up the situation. In 2014, the first national day celebrating the Constitution was instituted; on that very same day, the most censored word on the internet and Chinese social media was none other than 'Constitution'. There is no better means of demonstrating that the purpose of the law and its institutions is to serve the Chinese Communist Party, and not to guarantee citizens' rights. 'The reform of our legal system, an important part of the political system, plays a key role in the modernisation of the system and the State's governing capacities,' Xi declared on 7 January 2014, during the National Conference on Legal and Political Affairs.

> By reinforcing the leadership, promoting it in a coordinated fashion, and prioritising efficiency, we must accelerate the establishment of a socialist justice system defined by justice, efficiency, and authority with the aim of better maintaining the leadership of the Party, better demonstrating the characteristics of the

Chinese judicial system, as well as promoting social equity and justice.

Another consequence of Xi's 'closet' Legalism is his particular hatred of lawyers, whom he has managed to silence; notably those lawyers who, during the Hu Jintao years, started defending human rights, taking literally the government's promotion of a greater respect for the law as regularly outlined in its speeches. Victims of expropriations or misfeasance were less reluctant to go to court. But under Xi, the repression of lawyers has increased, and led to a large crackdown in July 2015, when 300 human rights lawyers and activists were arrested and questioned, and three legal firms raided by the police. While the majority were released in the weeks that followed, some were convicted. One year later, the authorities took new measures to reinforce their control over 22,000 legal practices. The latter were simply ordered to 'support the leadership of the Chinese Communist Party'. Political cells, which served as supervisory bodies, became compulsory.

For human rights organisations, these decisions were aimed at intimidating lawyers and keeping them from 'working independently and impartially', and also served to restrict free speech. The government went even further in its call to order when it demanded that practices dismiss any lawyers who discussed cases publicly or on social media. Law must serve government—yet another essential lesson from Legalism.

In January 2017, Zhou Qiang, China's top judge and president of the Supreme People's Court, made himself very clear to an assembly of magistrates in Beijing:

> We should resolutely resist erroneous Western ideas such as 'the separation of powers' and 'independence of the judiciary'. We need to oppose those who talk against the leadership of the Communist Party and attack the Chinese socialist system. We need to be ready to respond, to bring out our weapons and prepare for battle.

In short, while there are more references to Taoist proverbs than to Legalism in Xi Jinping's speeches, Legalism holds more sway in his intellectual universe. There is every reason to believe that he is personally inspired by Legalism, and that it is of great assistance in his countering of Western legal thought.

However, it is clear that the school of thought that features most prominently of all in Xi's speeches is Confucianism. It is fascinating for a Western observer to see the Chinese leader, heir to those who fought Confucian culture at the end of the nineteenth century, now including that same philosophy wholly and openly in his worldview.

7

COMRADE CONFUCIUS

Confucius is a thinker whom Xi Jinping cherishes, and he does not hesitate to show it. Less than a year after his accession to the highest public office, on 26 November 2013, the Chinese president travelled to Qufu, Confucius's birthplace, in the east of the country, setting the start of his mandate under the patronage of this illustrious figure.

During the trip, he took the time to meet with scholars at the Confucius Research Institute, founded in 1996 with the active support of the Jiang government. The Institute is housed in the former residence of the great philosopher's heirs—according to the authorities, in 2009 there were more than 2 million, recorded over eighty generations. At the entrance, Xi stopped for a minute before a table covered with books and periodicals. Two of them caught his eye: one was a commentary on Confucius' *Analects*, the other a collection of quotations from the master and his disciples. 'I want to read these two books carefully,' he said to the cohort of journalists in tow. This fleeting moment was swiftly seized upon by the propaganda machine. The same day, on the public television channel CCTV-13, a presenter recounted the incident with a smile on his face. This was undoubtedly good news—and a political message, of course. It was not hard for observers to see in this episode an additional sign of Confucius' long rehabilitation, in which Xi has played the role of catalyst.

It did not, then, come as a surprise when, in September 2014, the president took part in Confucius' 2,565[th] birthday celebrations. He even attended the Fifth Congress of the International Confucian Association. Before an audience already won-over, Xi gave a long speech lauding the 'son of Qufu'. He placed him in the pantheon of great men and praised his intellectual qualities:

> As an important component of traditional Chinese culture, the Confucian philosophy he created and the Confucian ideology established thereafter have exerted profound influences on Chinese civilisation. Along with other intellectual achievements that have been generated in the formulation and development of the Chinese nation, Confucianism recorded the Chinese nation's spiritual activities, rational thinking and cultural achievements in building their homeland, reflected spiritual pursuits of the Chinese nation, and provided a key source of nutrition for the survival and continuous growth of our nation. The Chinese civilisation has not only profoundly influenced China's own

development, but has also made significant contributions to the progress of human civilisation as a whole.

The reversal was complete: China's most famous sage, previously despised by Revolutionary Marxists who saw in his intellectual and political legacy one of the sources of the country's backwardness, was now rehabilitated, precisely because he has been deemed a resource of use in the 'development' and 'expansion' of China among the nations of the world. He is the figurehead of a comprehensive cultural diplomacy. It had been some years since Confucius' *Analects* first replaced Mao's *Little Red Book*. Since 2004 the Chinese government has bestowed the former's name on the cultural centres set up abroad along the lines of the Institut Français, the Instituto Cervantes and the Goethe Institute.

On that day in 2014, addressing an audience perfectly aware that the Communists had long discredited Confucius' work and thought, Xi assured them that the great thinker had truly benefitted the country. Nor had the Chinese Communists been the only ones to view Confucius in this light—the West also blamed him for the 'backwardness' of Chinese civilisation. The German sociologist Max Weber, for instance, attributed capitalism's failure to develop in China to a number of ideological factors, including Confucianism. It was almost a mantra that, as long as Confucius reigned supreme, there would be no move towards modernity. What is more, the young Chinese rebels of the early twentieth century, having subscribed to this widely shared conviction in the West, had boldly proclaimed that Confucius' 'shop' should close. 'The whole twentieth century was spent demolishing Confucius,' Anne Cheng, professor at the Collège de France and a specialist in the history of Chinese intellectual thought, claims:

> It even started at the end of the nineteenth century: it was at that time that the demolition of temples, be they dedicated to Confucius, ancestors, Taoist divinities or Buddha, began. Everything was swiftly secularised. Confucius became the target of all the modernising movements, and then, of course, of the Maoist regime, built on the clean slate it called into being. That meant that everything reminiscent of the old society, be it Confucian, ritualistic, family-oriented, had to be destroyed.

Based on the texts of the philosopher, who had lived in the 'Spring and Autumn period' between the sixth and fifth centuries BCE, contemporaneous with the pre-Socratics, Confucianism was the backbone of the Imperial system. All children, century after century, learned the great texts at school, and the selection of Imperial civil servants was based on knowledge of the Confucian corpus. The latter was established only four centuries after the philosopher's death, during the Han dynasty. His teachings, compiled in works written by his disciples and later debated in other books by his successors, became the Empire's official doctrine. Five works dating back to the first millennium BCE, which recorded the word of the 'saints' and sages, became the 'Five Classics': a poetry anthology (*Book of Songs*); a compilation of political texts (*Book of Documents*); a treaty on divination (*Yijing*); a collection of ritual prescriptions (*Book of Rites*); and a historical chronicle (*Spring and Autumn Annals*). Confucius was 'beatified' during the same period, achieving sage status, to the point that the man he had been was forgotten. As Anne Cheng explains in the preface to her translation of Confucius' *Analects*— his most famous work, with an influence in East Asia similar to that of the Bible in Christian Europe—he is probably best imagined as an 'educator, surrounded by a small group of loyal disciples'. 'The Confucian school,' she continues, 'must have started out as a group of friends who enjoyed debating the questions of their time, since most of them would have been actively involved in the political life of their country.'

Confucius' central teaching resides in the importance given to the *Dao*, or *Tao*—the path of the Ancients, of the kings of Antiquity, that sovereigns must follow: 'I transmit but do not innovate; I am truthful in what I say and devoted to Antiquity,' he says. In terms of moral teachings, there are four cardinal notions: humanity, justice, rites, and wisdom. The philosopher in fact melds moral wisdom and political ideals. Thus, a good man, particularly a sovereign, must behave in exemplary fashion. The theorists of the Imperial order saw this as a call for obedience: to the emperor, to the father, to the master. On the contrary, other thinkers will see in it the opportunity to contest all unjust authority. Obedience on the one hand, resistance on the other—Confucius' legacy has and will continue to be exploited, subverted, and caricatured. 'Before the consolidation of Manchu power [1644–1911], what we call Confucianism was more frequently used as a weapon by the opposition than as an official ideology,' sinologist Jacques Gernet points out.

This heritage, handed down over two millennia, was first challenged following the clash with Western powers at the end of the nineteenth century. Towards the end of the Qing dynasty—China's last—functionaries proved themselves very much aware of the need to adapt to changing times and to engage with Western ideas that were spreading among the elite. To avoid the collapse of their world, and especially the collapse of the imperial system, they embarked on a series of reforms. Yet they were inspired by, rather than deviating from, Confucian ideology. They even put Confucius on a pedestal, a little like the establishment of Shinto in Japan in response to the Western threat during the Meiji era (1868–1912). Shinto, which had only been a set of beliefs until that point, became the official religion of a state centred on the emperor. The consequent unification of the country led to a beneficial modernisation, which allowed the country to resist the Western 'devils'.

One of the most renowned Chinese reformers, Kang Youwei (1858–1927), was convinced that China could do the same with Confucianism. He regretted the triumph of 'laxity and procrastination' that was leading the empire to its doom and allowing foreigners to impose their diktats. It was imperative for Confucianism to be restored to its former glory, he pointed out in a petition to the emperor. The text was written at a painful time for China. Its navy had suffered a heavy defeat against the Japanese in February 1895, which had led to the humiliating Shimonoseki treaty. Beijing was made to renounce all sovereignty over Korea, and to cede Taiwan, the Ryukyu archipelago, and the Liaodong peninsula in north-eastern China.

Kang Youwei let his rage get the better of him: 'Confucian knowledge can be used to govern the country. But few are those who can promote it. This is why the perverse doctrines of foreign savages have spread and deceived the people. Is it not shameful that one can barely find a Confucian temple in each prefecture, while churches are opening all over the country like pawns on a chess-board?' To organise the Chinese response, he suggested that Confucianism be instated as the 'state religion' (*guojiao*). He even invented a neologism: Confucianism in his works is termed *kongjiao*, or 'Kong's religion'—Confucius being a Latinised form of the sage's Mandarin name, Kong Fuzi. In July 1898, he sent a further petition to the emperor. He had had another idea: to establish a calendar that would start on the date of Confucius' birth, rather than being based on dynastic reigns. He also suggested instituting a Confucian mass, at which priests would read the classical texts. After all, explains Kang's disciple Chen Huanzhang, like Christianity, Confucianism had 'ceremonial vestments, a canon, rules, a liturgy, a theology featuring a single god and the immortality of the soul, a doctrine on retribution, schools, temples, and holy sites'.

This Christian-inspired 'Confucian extremism' was never implemented. The Parliament of the young Republic of China twice rejected a project aiming at establishing Confucianism as the state religion, once in 1913 and again in 1916. During the same period, the opposition were just as adamant in their complete rejection of Confucianism. In 1919, students wishing to extricate their country from its backwardness called 'Mr Science and Mr Democracy' to their defence against Master Confucius.

Confucianism's most virulent critic was the writer Lu Xun (1881–1936), a renowned intellectual who rejected traditionalist China and whose writings, in particular his fiction, heavily influenced the modernisers. Indeed, it is he whom Revolutionaries, including Mao Zedong himself, claimed as their inspiration. Under Mao, Confucianism was demonised, considered one of the 'Four Olds'—old ideas, old culture, old customs, and old habits—that had to eradicated from Chinese culture by the Red Guards. In 1966, the Great Helmsman symbolically named Lu Xun, who had died thirty years earlier, 'Commander-in-Chief of China's Cultural Revolution'. In 1974, he launched the 'Criticise Lin and Confucius' campaign. The targets were his former number two, Lin Biao, who died in a plane accident after a failed coup attempt, and the ancient philosopher. The founder of the People's Republic of China pursued his vendetta against Master Kong to the end of his days.

With this tormented history in mind, one realises the full scale of the reversal conducted by the current communist leadership. In reclaiming the Confucian legacy, the regime is breaking away from a long political tradition associated with modernity. In a November 2013 speech, Xi Jinping went even further in this rehabilitation, associating Karl Marx unequivocally with Confucius. Explaining his intentions for leadership before the Central Committee of the Chinese Communist Party, he affirmed that, at the start of the twenty-first century, 'Socialism with Chinese characteristics' was as much in need of 'social harmony' as it was of 'communist energy'.

Xi refers to Confucius' proverbs much more frequently and extensively than his predecessors did. But Deng Xiaoping and Hu Jintao were no less responsible for this appropriation—they paved the way for it. As we have seen, Confucian values, which are deeply rooted in Chinese culture, can be used to maintain order and support leaders in their quest for stability. Deng, for instance, referred to a 'moderately prosperous society' (*xiaokang shehui*, an expression from the *Book of Rites*), a society from which poverty would have been eradicated. Xi Jinping also elaborated on this idea in a speech on Confucius's 2,565[th] birthday:

> The Chinese people are working hard to fulfil their 'twin centennial goals', one of which is the concept of *xiaokang*, or a relatively well-off life, an ideal state of society the Chinese nation has been seeking since ancient times, which originated from the *Book of Rites*. Using the concept *xiaokang* in defining a national development goal not only conforms to the reality of the country's development but is also conducive to mustering the broadest public understanding and support.

According to Xi, this 'relatively well-off life' will have been reached by the year 2020.

As for Hu, he had promoted the 'harmonious society', a concept heavily influenced by Confucianism—the quest for 'harmony' (*hexie*) being a fundamental element of Confucius' philosophy. On 4 March 2006, during a meeting at the Chinese People's Political Consultative Conference, he referred to the 'socialist concepts of honour and disgrace' (*shehuizhuyi rongruguan*) and listed the 'eight honours and eight disgraces'. To a Chinese audience, these terms are obvious references to the Confucian corpus. Moreover, a list of honours was displayed all over the country and in every school:

Love the country; do it no harm.
Serve the people; do no disservice.
Follow science; discard ignorance.
Be diligent; not indolent.
Be united, help each other; make no gains at other's
  expense.
Be honest and trustworthy; do not spend ethics for
  profits.
Be disciplined and law-abiding; not chaotic and
  lawless.
Live plainly, struggle hard; do not wallow in luxuries
  and pleasures.

This text could have been written before the Marxist regime came to power. It draws on lessons of ancestral wisdom. *The People's Daily*, the Party newspaper, had defended the need for these lessons in morality by arguing that 'children need to be inspired by social practices, to live in a virtuous and harmonious environment with new morals. Since children are naturally playful and active, we must ensure that they learn while having fun and by distinguishing honour from disgrace.' Xi has adopted this moralistic vision aimed at educating Chinese youth, using it in his anti-corruption campaign.

The alliance of Confucianism and Marxism, which defies logic to an outside observer, is probably a means of compensating for the regime's weaknesses. Since Mao's death, the Party has lost the impetus of the 'permanent revolution'. Today, it also on the verge of losing its double-digit growth rate. Xi must build a new economic model. The one that was launched at the end of the 1970s, and allowed China to become the world's second-largest economic power, is on its last legs. A period of transition, and consequently of potential instability, lies ahead. China's leaders are worried about the rise of inequality and of social tension in the country, and they need a coherent discourse to deal with these issues. To construct it, Xi has decided to preserve the state's Marxist foundations (the principle of fighting against severe social inequalities), to glorify Nationalism (as we shall see further on), and to rely on traditions. 'China's wonderful traditional culture', in which he revels, has become something that generates both order and respect; something in which he hopes to find the cement of a new cohesion.

This is all the more necessary given one of the consequences of the country's rapid growth: the disorientation of Chinese youth. The rise of living standards combined with the one-child policy has led to what is being called within China itself a 'moral crisis': the younger generations are undermined by excessive consumerism. 'Official discourse pushes these issues, namely the population's crisis of confidence, the worship of money, and so on,' points out Sébastien Billioud, professor of Chinese studies at the University Paris-Diderot. 'This is how the leadership perceives the current moral crisis. In this context, the moralising discourse of traditional culture has an important role to play, in promoting filial piety, for instance.' After thirty years of unbridled economic growth and spiritual vacuum, Confucius has been summoned to the rescue to heal Chinese society's ills.

But the powers that be are not the only ones responsible for this revival of Confucianism in China. Even before the Party changed course, 'Confucius fever' had taken hold of the country in the 2000s. Is this the by-product of an excessively materialistic society? Chinese people appeared anxious to return to their roots as well as to find spiritual nourishment. 'Academies'—in other words, Confucian private schools—opened in some regions, under the auspices of local authorities. In 2007, I visited one of these schools, which had just opened in suburban Beijing. 'Confucius' teachings are the first thing we teach children,' the school's director, Feng Zhe, explained to me. Around fifty boys and girls under the age of fourteen attended this school, housed grandly in a converted pavilion. 'Each child must recite Confucian texts a thousand times until it is committed to memory,' the director claimed, swiftly emphasising that this was done under the aegis of the Chinese Communist Party: 'The concept of scientific development and the idea of a harmonious society promoted by the government come from Chinese traditional culture.' He added: 'We hope our students will become cultural ambassadors for China throughout the world.' Mr Feng anticipated that within ten years there would be 10,000 such schools all over the country.

At the same time, Yu Dan, professor of communication at Beijing Normal University, was riding the wave. After making Confucius' *Analects* accessible to the general public in a series broadcast on state television, she published *Confucius from the Heart* (*Lunyu xinde*, or 'Reflections on the Analects'). Millions of copies were sold, and Yu became a celebrity. Her secret? She made Confucius a 'feel-good' author, a cross between self-fulfilment, New Age spirituality, and meditation. For Daniel Bell, a Beijing-based Canadian political scientist, Yu Dan makes her readers feel proud about their cultural heritage 'while showing that it's compatible with the requirements of modern life'. For instance, she writes,

> What we can learn from Confucius today is not the 'Confucian Learning' set out by Emperor Wu; it is not the solemn, dignified, ritualized 'Confucian religion' that stands alongside Taoism and Buddhism in China; nor is it the Confucianism of the scholars, full of deep argumentation and fettered by textual research. What we can take away from the *Analects* of Confucius are the simple truths that every person knows in his or her heart, though they may not let them out through their mouths.

She even refers to the Great Helmsman: 'The words of Chairman Mao in response to Comrade Guo Moruo: "Seize every moment, for ten thousand years are too long" could not be more appropriate today. If ten thousand years are too long, so too are seventy.' And so, it seems, we must all read Confucius.

Yu Dan's interpretation is obviously completely depoliticised—in the West her book has been classified by publishers and booksellers as falling under 'spirituality' and 'personal well-being'—which explains the criticism of some specialists. 'These books written for the general public exploit media and social phenomena found in television shows aimed at an urban middle-class audience,' Anne Cheng argues.

> Ten million copies of this book have already been sold. It rightly incurred the wrath of many academics who accused Yu Dan of sucking the life out of the *Analects* by ignoring certain passages where Confucius criticises the politicians of his time, and the questions these passages may raise and that have in fact been raised by many previous readings of Chinese culture. Behind the guise of brevity and simplicity hides a consensual and conservative reading that, according to some, reduces Confucius' great humanist message to 'chicken soup for the soul', and which conforms entirely to the official discourse on social harmony.

Apart from Yu Dan's bestseller, the restoration of the Temple of Confucius in Beijing is another sign of the times. A statue of the master, hands on his chest, sits at the entrance, close to the tablets where the names of scholars who have passed their exams are engraved. Numbers increase year on year among parents and students who visit the temple before exam season to pay homage to the master—at the same location where their predecessors, the Red Guards, had been unleashed on the statues and sacred tablets. Groups of visitors from all over the country also flock there; the temple is a favourite stop on any tour of the capital, alongside the Mao Mausoleum in the city centre, and Tiananmen Square. In an irony of history, two former enemies have been reunited by ideology and leisure.

This wave of Confucian fervour is not just a passing fad. It probably expresses a deep-seated demand within Chinese society. 'In the 2000s, a popular form of Confucianism developed relatively independently of the elites,' confirms Sébastien Billioud. 'In 2010, there was a rapid influx of political, economic, and intellectual elites who tried to recuperate the movement.' But what about Xi's motives? Is his show of interest in Confucius not simply a way for him to keep 'in touch' with the people? He must keep pace with Chinese society's internal vitality. It would be the very limit for a Communist Party claiming to be the avant-garde to jump on a train that had already left the station.

Much of the Confucius craze is open to conjecture, but certain motivations for the regime are explicit. In his visit to the sage's birthplace at Qufu in 2013, Xi discussed at length his references to Confucius, and justified them by pointing out the importance of celebrating thousands of years of culture:

> In his speeches, comrade Mao Zedong used many of the ideas of Confucius, the Confucian school and the

Hundred Schools of Thought. I also quote a lot from Confucius in my speeches. These famous words and principles have been handed down across more than two thousand years of history and experiment, and today we see the value of Confucius' thought more clearly. In history, many respected Confucius, many opposed Confucius, and many resented Confucius, there were many political twists and turns, but now we see clearly, and we have reached a consensus on the essence of Confucian thought. Confucius has had a great influence on the thinking of the civilized progress of humanity, and the sinification of Marxism. To handle China's affairs well, we must use methods that are consistent with conditions in China. ... We should think of Confucius' thought in terms of historical materialism; today's China is a product of China's history, and it should adhere to this attitude, adhere to Marxist methods, adopt a Marxist attitude in the study of Confucius, Confucianism and traditional culture.

The aim, Xi continues, is to 'advance the building of a socialist core value system, and develop and expand the things essential to traditional culture. ... I have come to Qufu this time to send a message: we must vigorously expand and develop China's traditional culture.' The propaganda apparatus has also played its role in this drive to return to tradition, underlining Xi's informed use of Confucius's *Analects* (*Lunyu*), but also of the classics in general. In 2015 a book was released listing all of Xi's references to classical texts in his speeches, *Xi*

Jinping yong dan ('Xi Jinping knows the classics'). An English-language version was even published in the United States.

In 2014, another speech indicated the link between the revival of Confucianism and a newly-found national pride, when Xi expressed to teachers his opposition to the withdrawal of 'classical poetry and texts' from schoolbooks. On the contrary, he exclaimed, 'the classics should be ingrained in students' minds and become the cultural genes of Chinese people.' Xi had also defended the bedrock of Chinese culture during his visit to Qufu: 'If we look at the issue of "human rights" for instance, many Western countries have now abolished the death penalty, but if abolition were submitted to a referendum in China, then many ordinary Chinese would not approve of it. ... I told the Greek Prime Minister, "your 'democracy' comes from ancient Greece and ancient Rome, that is your tradition. We have our own tradition."' With such statements, Xi—a communist leader—is defending something that Maoism was built to oppose: ancestral laws, which conveniently justify national particularism.

Xi is aware that, if he is to glorify nationalist sentiment, he must be able to offer the narrative of a specifically 'Chinese history'. Traditional culture can prove very useful in this context. The dean of the Tsinghua Academy of Chinese Learning in Beijing, Chen Lai, believes that the Confucian revival is closely linked to the 'Chinese revival':

The ideological impetus from the government defines the whole framework, the role of the intellectual is decisive, cultural life prepares the terrain; but the most fundamental condition for the Confucian renewal resides in the renewal and re-emergence of the nation itself. In other words, the success of Chinese modernisation and the pace of economic development are the fundamental conditions for Confucian renewal. ... Once the modernisation process enters the stage of fast-paced development and the economy begins to grow successfully, the people's cultural self-confidence gradually recovers, resulting in a stronger sense of cultural identity. ... The contemporary *guoxue* [traditional China studies] craze signals an awakening in the nation's self-consciousness as well as an increase in its self-esteem and self-confidence. It has fostered a national cultural awareness and played an important role in a major revival of the Chinese nation. This is how national renewal at this point in history plays a fundamental role in Confucian renewal.

But which type of Confucianism does Chen mean? Certainly not the same Confucianism that had structured the society of Imperial China. Much like its popular incarnation, the Chinese Communist Party's brand of Confucianism has erased its most controversial aspects. There was never any question of rehabilitating the figure of the intellectual who dares criticise the emperor on pain of death. There's also no mention in Party Confucianism of Huang Zongxi, a seventeenth-century intellectual who attacked the ruling Ming dynasty in his book. 'Confucianism today is obviously very different,' Sébastien Billioud explains. 'In the last days of the empire, it was all-embracing, homogenising. Since then, it has only continued to perpetuate itself in a fragmentary way, under the guise of religious projects, philosophical projects, ideological projects and so on.'

The ideology used by the Party today serves to advance a type of 'paternalist authoritarianism', according to Anne Cheng. 'And so the leaders can say: China is not a dictatorship, nor an authoritarian regime, it is a Confucian regime.' For Sébastien Billioud, Xi makes strategic use of traditional culture. Noting that Xi often refers to 'simple' concepts, such as filial piety, he suggests:

> Today, traditional culture associated with education serves to contribute to moralisation, social stability, uplifting of the *suzhi*—the quality of [Chinese] citizens. For there is always the idea that humankind is malleable and that *suzhi* can be improved. But all this remains in the realm of the symbolic. Classical texts are certainly used to educative ends, but there is little evidence to support the idea that there is a coherent use of a corpus of Confucian doctrine.

Xi's cursory references to Confucius's classical texts are obviously not made as part of some in-depth theoretical reflection. They are used as maxims to support his gestures and explain his actions within the framework of an 'enlightened dictatorship'. In a speech given in March

2013 for the eightieth anniversary of the Central Party School, he made use of a raft of quotes. To offer just two: 'Be the first to feel concern about the country and the last to enjoy oneself' (Fan Zhongyan, a politician and writer from the Northern Song dynasty, who lived between 989 and 1,052 and advocated a new Confucian ideal); 'The one who has decided to give up on life to serve the state cannot retreat before misfortune' (Lin Zexu, 1785–1850, a high-ranking civil servant of the Qing dynasty who fought against the Opium trade). 'All these maxims,' Xi declared, 'embody the culture and spirit of the Chinese nation. We must seek inspiration from them and illustrate them brilliantly!' As in the other Confucian references we've seen, quoting these proverbs serve to create a soothing tone of discourse.

Some Confucian philosophers are not fooled, and have called upon the regime to go even further and return to a real political Confucianism, in the tradition of Dong Zhongshu (179–04 BCE), an intellectual who lived during the Western Han dynasty, when Confucianism was instituted as the official state ideology. One of the most renowned contemporary Confucian scholars is Jiang Qing, a professor who opened a Confucian academy in Guiyang. With Daniel Bell, the Canadian political scientist at Tsinghua University, he has called for a 'Confucian constitution' and the establishment of an all-new tri-cameral parliamentary system: with a 'house of exemplary personalities [house of *ru* or scholars]', a 'house of the nation', and a 'house of the people'.

The house of scholars, which represents the legitimacy of 'heaven', would be presided over by a 'an academic or renowned scholar'; the house of the nation, which represents the legitimacy of the 'earth' (historical and cultural wisdom), would be led by a 'direct descendant of Confucius'; and the house of the people by somebody elected or designated by representatives of professional organisations. 'To avoid political gridlock that may arise as a result of conflicts between the three houses of parliament,' the two authors write, 'a bill must pass at least two of the houses to become law. The priority of sacred legitimacy is expressed in the veto power exercised by the House of *Ru* ... the power of the *ru* is restrained by the other two houses. For instance, if they propose a bill restricting religious freedom, the People and the Nation will oppose it and it cannot become law.'

Others have suggested, quite straightforwardly, a merging of Marxism and Confucianism. This is the case of Gan Yang, an intellectual born in 1952 and educated in the United States who had been a liberal. However, he has since radically changed his views and become one of the main figures of the 'New Left', which is critical of liberalism and democracy. In a text published in 2009, on the sixtieth anniversary of the People's Republic, Gan pointed out that contemporary China needed to reconcile traditional Confucian culture, which particularly favours familial ties; Maoism, which sets great store by social equality and justice; and Deng Xiaoping's reforms, which have given way to the market. This is known as the 'three traditions' concept. Gan explained it to a journalist of the Chinese newspaper *21ˢᵗ Century Business Herald*:

> There are currently three traditions in China. The first is a tradition shaped by twenty-five years of reforms: even if this may seem like a short period of time, the reforms and the opening-up policy shaped many concepts, including many new ones, and this is deeply ingrained in the people's psyche ... This tradition spread thanks to the establishment of many concepts inspired by market forces, such as those of liberty, rights, etc. Another tradition goes back to the foundation of the People's Republic of China, and is the product of the Mao Zedong era, which focuses on the attention given to equality and justice. Finally, there is the tradition of Chinese civilisation that dates back several thousands of years, and which is more often known as traditional Chinese culture or Confucian culture. It is difficult to define exactly, but in the Chinese people's daily lives it often manifests itself as an awareness of human relations and a sensitivity to nostalgia for the motherland.

Five years later, Gan Yang had developed his theory further: 'In essence, the People's Republic of China is a Confucian socialist republic. Therein lies the deeper meaning of the Chinese reforms: to further and develop the content of such a republic; that is the aim of the twenty-first century.' He also insists that the thirty years of reforms and opening-up policy (1979–2000) should not be used to criticise the three decades of Maoism, and vice versa. Even if there are unavoidable tensions between the three traditions, Gan believes that only through their fusion can China find its path. 'Only by insisting upon the tradition of socialism and classical culture can China develop liberalism,' points out Zhou Lian, professor of Oriental philosophy at the People's University (Beijing). This point of view resembles that of Xi himself. He wishes to combine the 'three traditions': (i) that of Mao, the 'father of the nation'; (ii) that of Xi Zhongxun, his own father and a key figure of the Deng reforms, whom Xi honoured in official ceremonies marking his birth centenary in October 2013; and finally (iii) the traditional culture Xi constantly praises.

8

CULTURE WARS

In April 2013, a month after Xi Jinping became president, a text was secretly distributed within the Party. State media did not mention it. Known as 'Document 9' (the Central Committee's ninth report that year), its official title is 'Communiqué on the Current State of the Ideological Sphere'. The Western media only found out about this document when the dissident Chinese website Mingjing published its leaked contents in September 2013. This text is vitally important, because it is a detailed outline of Xi's programme. It sheds striking light on the beginning of his presidency, a crucial period during which he made his mark. In fact, by the end of 2013, observers—noting Xi's obvious desire to concentrate all powers within his own person—had stopped comparing him with Gorbachev and were using the Mao Zedong analogy instead. The authorities suspected Chinese journalist Gao Yu, who had already been imprisoned for over a year after Tiananmen and for six years in the '90s, of leaking Document 9 to Mingjing. In April 2015 she was sentenced to seven years' imprisonment for divulging state secrets. Such a strict verdict underlined the importance of Document 9 to the regime.

This very sensitive and explosive report—written by Xi himself, some say—is entirely devoted to study of the 'ideological sphere'. Beijing's new strongman, obsessed by the Soviet experience, is convinced that 'hostile forces', whether internal or Western, must be contained. The document underscores this 'intense struggle' against 'false ideological trends, positions, and activities'. Seven of these are listed explicitly: 'Western Constitutional Democracy', 'universal values', 'civil society', 'neoliberalism', 'the West's idea of journalism', 'historical nihilism', and the critique of 'Socialism with Chinese characteristics'.

These 'false trends' deserve to be looked at in more detail. First of all, 'Western Constitutional Democracy', whose followers supposedly seek to undermine the 'Socialism with Chinese characteristics system of governance': its aims, according to Document 9, are 'the separation of powers, the multi-party system, general elections, an independent judiciary, [and] a national army'. The Chinese people had never forgotten the dream of democracy, which had recently regained currency and was by no means innocuous. Thus far, the Document's analysis is correct. In 2012 opponents of the regime had used the thirtieth anniversary of the 1982 Constitution's adoption as an excuse to call the government's bluff. Many of these opponents were part of the civil and legal rights movement developed during the Hu presidency (2003–12), which also included in its ranks those known as the 'barefoot lawyers', and members of the 'New Citizens' Movement' (*gongmen*), founded in 2010 by legal experts such as the academic Xu Zhiyong. These dissidents' strategy involved targeting Party leaders and accusing them of placing themselves above the Constitution. Some even used the slogan 'constitutional dream' as a subversion of the 'Chinese dream'. For the authors of Document 9, therefore, ideas of genuine constitutional democracy are used to undermine the Party's leadership, 'to abolish the People's democracy', 'negate our country's constitution as well as our established system and principles, and push towards a change of allegiance by bringing Western political systems to China.'

The second danger outlined in the document is the promotion of 'universal values'. Simply put: those who wish to 'claim that the West's value system defies time and space, transcends nation and class, and applies to all humanity' are in fact adversaries—this can be read as a direct attack on intellectuals influenced by liberalism. Their hostility and dishonesty can be seen 'in their distortion of the Party's own promotion of democracy, freedom, equality, justice, rule of law, and other such values'. For instance, Document 9 asserted, these enemies insist that Western values are 'the prevailing norm for all human civilisation, that only when China accepts Western values will it have a future, and that Reform and Opening-Up is just a process of gradually accepting universal rights.' The Document's authors warned against such slogans, which aimed 'to obscure the essential differences between the West's value system and the value system we advocate'.

The third peril detailed in Document 9 is the promotion of 'civil society'. Civil society is described as a socio-political theory that originated in the West, and which asserts that 'individual rights are paramount' in the social sphere—a proposition close to scandalous in the Party leaders' eyes. Yet, 'for the past few years, the idea of civil society has been adopted by Western anti-China forces and used as a political tool'. Its advocates thus claim that 'building a civil society in China is a precondition for the protection of individual rights and forms the basis for the realisation of constitutional democracy.' Moreover, viewing civil society 'as a magic bullet for advancing social management at the local level', these hostile forces have launched 'all kinds of so-called citizens' movements'. Their objective is clear: to distance the Party from the leadership of the masses at a local level. And 'their advocacy is becoming a serious form of political opposition'.

The fourth danger has to do with economics. According to Document 9, Westerners, led by the United States, seek to impose a neo-liberal agenda in China, under the guise of 'globalisation'. Actively promoting 'market omnipotence theory', such neo-liberals claim that 'our country's macroeconomic control is strangling the market's efficiency and vitality'. Worse still, these same Westerners are against public ownership, 'arguing that China's state-owned enterprises are "national monopolies", inefficient, and disruptive of the market economy, and should undergo "comprehensive privatisation."' This is obviously an intolerable means of weakening government control.

The fifth peril is the West's idea of journalism, which defies 'the principle of China'. This hallowed principle follows a simple logic: the media and all means of publication are bound by Party discipline. By defining media as 'society's public instrument', the 'hostile forces' are in fact attacking 'the Marxist view of news'. More shocking still, they are 'slandering our country's efforts to improve internet management by calling them a crackdown on the internet'. We have already looked at 'historical nihilism' in Chapter 4; the final danger facing China is the questioning of the 'socialist nature of "Socialism with Chinese characteristics"'. This last point, which is no small thing, comes across in Document 9 as truly worrisome:

> [Some] question whether or not what China is doing now is still truly socialism, or they just call it 'capitalist socialism', 'state capitalism', or 'new bureaucratic capitalism'. Others say 'reform is still distant and hasn't been realised', or that 'reform of the political system lags

behind and obstructs reform of the economy.' They bang on about how we should use Western standards to achieve so-called 'thorough reform' ... These mistaken views and ideas exist in great numbers in overseas media and reactionary publications.

In short, Western forces and internal 'dissidents' use every means available to infiltrate the ideological sphere. How, exactly? Document 9 has an explanation for this, too: through 'Western embassies, consulates, media operations, and NGOs operating inside China under various covers'. The text concludes, 'In the face of these threats, we must not let down our guard or decrease our vigilance.'

It is important to dwell on this text, which, as firm as it is paranoid, provides one of the keys to understanding Xi's policies—especially his attitude towards the media. This is one of the areas in which his influence is particularly visible. Xi closed the door on the brief period under Hu, particularly during the 2008 Beijing Olympics, when it seemed that China would gain true freedom of speech, with an impetus similar to the Russian *glasnost*. Newspapers and television companies had pushed back censorship; comprehensive investigations had exposed local scandals; and the boom in internet and social media use had opened public forums.

To describe Xi's takeover, a photograph is worth a thousand words. Xi is smiling, sitting in the presenter's chair of the seven o'clock news, the country's most popular news programme for the past forty years. His message is clear, and further proof of his omnipotence: the leader dictates the news. This picture was taken in 2016, during a presidential visit to the headquarters of *The People's Daily* and Xinhua, the official news agency, on his way to the studios of powerful state broadcaster CCTV. Three media outlets in one day—Xi is particularly keen on 'the work of guiding public opinion', as he described it on that occasion. 'The media run by the party and the government are on the propaganda front and must have the Party as their family name. They should also stick to guiding public opinion on the correct path in every aspect and stage of their work,' he declared.

The phrase 'have the Party as their family name', provoked indignant reactions on the internet. The charge was led by property developer Ren Zhiqiang, Party member and eminent celebrity blogger with 37 million followers. Nicknamed 'The Cannon' for his searing critiques, he published a series of posts on his Weibo account, arguing that the media belong to all of China, not just the Party: 'Since when has the people's government been turned into the Party's government? Is their money the Party's? Don't waste taxpayers' money on things that do not provide them with services.' The cunning Ren, despite belonging to the 'red aristocracy'—his father was vice-minister of commerce in 1970—was promptly silenced, his Weibo account deleted by the 'Cyberspace administration'. Mimicking Western online communities' self-monitoring procedures, its spokesperson declared in a statement: 'Internet users have reported that Ren Zhiqiang's account had been continuously publishing illegal information, and the impact was vile.' Moreover, the Party threatened to expel him, and suspended him for a year. His crime was opposing the Party and 'losing the Party spirit'.

Xi Jinping expressed this obsession with control over the media very early on in his career; one might say that he had identified it even then as the most vital weapon of all. In May 1989, when the pro-democracy protests disrupted the life of the country and paralysed the heart of the capital in Tiananmen Square, Xi held a government post in the southern province of Fujian, 1,000 kilometres away. In response to these 'political troubles', he called a meeting on 'the work of reporting'. He was already advocating firm handling of the media: 'Reporters must feel the pulse of their time, recognise the role of the news, understand that they are the spokespersons of the Party and the people. Their main task is to reflect and guide public opinion.'

As soon as he came to power in early 2013, Xi took it upon himself to remind journalists of their mission. He launched a 'movement of education of the Marxist journalistic vision' at the state broadcaster CCTV. Meetings and workshops were organised throughout the year to address the topics of 'conviction, ideals, [and] responsibility'. 'New gatherers' were reminded of the importance of 'supervising public opinion'. They were asked to develop 'a journalism of solutions and progress', designed to protect 'the interests of the popular masses'. During a stock-taking meeting in October 2013 in Beijing, Kang Wei, one of the celebrity presenters of the seven o'clock evening news, estimated that the movement had led to a 'heightened awareness of the link between the Party, the country, and the people, and a better understanding of what it meant to be a journalist'. It was the price to pay for staying in the Party's favour.

Xi also pays particular attention to internet control. He deals with this issue much as he does with free speech: by proving more inflexible than his predecessors. Despite increasing pressure, Xi maintains a blocking policy against the American tech giants, such as Google and Facebook. He has remained immune to the charms of *Lianpu* (Facebook in Mandarin). The social network was first banned in China in 2009 during protests in the Muslim province of Xinjiang, which then spread to the rest of the country. Since, it has been used as a mobilisation tool in the 'Arab Springs', and promoted—perhaps a bit hastily—as the key to democratisation. This was enough for it to be identified in Document 9 as a tool of the 'hostile forces' seeking to undermine China.

Yet, officially, Xi approves of digital technologies—specifically, Chinese ones. In a speech given on 19 April 2016 at the Work Conference on Cybersecurity and Informatisation to internet entrepreneurs, members of the military, and researchers in cybersecurity, Xi underlined that Chinese Communist Party cadres had to be present online in order to face the criticisms and suggestions of public opinion:

> I have often stressed that we must lock power into a cage of rules, and one important method is giving rein to the role of public opinion supervision including internet supervision ... We should not only welcome internet supervision, regardless of whether it is aimed at Party and government work or at an individual leading cadre, regardless of whether it is put gently and mildly or is a hurtful truth, but we must earnestly research and adopt it.

For 'wherever the masses are, there our leading cadres must go,' he said. One of those in the audience was Jack Ma, director of Alibaba, the top e-commerce company in China. Alibaba is just one of the 'Chinese giants' that Beijing, in its effort to build a digital economy, favours over foreign competition. Other figures of the Chinese web economy were also present, such as Huawei's director-general Ren Zhengfei; Lei Jun, founder of the mobile telephone maker Xiaomi; and Robin Li, the creator of Baidu, China's most popular search engine.

These big Chinese companies are developing projects that align with the government's plans to establish a 'social credit' system rating businesses and citizens, to prevent fraud and counterfeiting. An official document published in 2014 explains that the scheme will 'ensure that those keeping trust receive benefit in all respects, and those breaking trust meet with difficulty at every step.' Rights advocates saw this as an attempt at establishing a society of control through smartphones, a Chinese 'Big Brother'. They argue that the scheme aims to evaluate individuals based on 'a number of criteria, from your behaviour on public transport to whether or not you visit your parents,' explains Mareike Ohlberg, analyst at the Mercator Institute for China Studies, an independent research institute based in Berlin.

In reality, this approach is the result of lengthy planning, including on the technical side. Séverine Arsène, an expert on the internet in China, points out that, as early as the end of the 1990s, the Chinese had been pioneers in the quest to control this virtual space from which independent voices could emerge. She explains:

> The Chinese looked for a means of participating in it without taking any political risks—using a system of domain names as a filter. They were the first to do so. This model spread to other countries—Iran, Tunisia, Libya (there thanks to French companies such as Qosmos or Amesys). In fact, the filtering of data happens in almost every country in the world, even in democracies, for reasons that are sometimes justified, as long as they respect the rule of law.

Xi wants to build a 'healthy and clean cyberspace', in other words a cyberspace under his control To justify it, he uses a surprisingly bucolic metaphor, cited here in its entirety:

Cyberspace is a common spiritual garden for hundreds of millions of people. Having a clear sky and crisp air, having a good ecology in cyberspace conforms to the people's interests. A pestilent atmosphere and a deteriorating ecology in cyberspace do not conform to the people's interest. No one would be willing to live in a space that is full of falsehoods, fraud, attacks, jeering, terror, sex, and violence. The internet is not a land outside the law. The use of the internet to play up subversion of the national regime, to stir up religious extremism, to propagate ethnic separatist thought, to instigate violent and terrorist activities—these acts must be firmly curbed and attacked, we absolutely cannot let them have their way. The use of networks to engage in fraudulent activities, to disseminate sexual material, to engage in personal attacks, to sell illegal goods and so on, these words and deeds must also be firmly brought under control; we also absolutely cannot let them have their way. There isn't any country that would permit such acts to spread unchecked. We must, with an attitude of responsibility towards society and responsibility towards the people, lawfully strengthen governance in cyberspace, strengthen the construction of online content, strengthen online positive propaganda, foster a positive, healthy, upward and benevolent online culture, use the core socialist values and the excellent achievements of human civilisation to nourish people's hearts and nourish society, ensure that positive energy is plentiful, that the main melody soars, and that a cyberspace with a crisp wind and a correct air is created for all those online, especially the young.

Creating a good public opinion environment online does not mean that there can only be one voice or one tune, but it means that we cannot fiddle with right and wrong, confound black and white, spread rumours to create trouble, break the law and commit crime; we cannot exceed the boundaries of the Constitution and the laws.

In other words, Xi wants to build the internet in Noddy-land.

This context of strict control and censorship explains why the reception of foreign, and specifically American, economic actors is subject to certain conditions, and why those who sought to conquer the Chinese market in the past have repeatedly failed. Google and Yahoo! tried to get a foothold but were unsuccessful. Mark Zuckerberg also wants to break through. Despite criticism, he makes regular overtures to Beijing, a major one being his undertaking to learn Mandarin, which he had the chance to practise when he met Xi Jinping in Seattle in September 2015. He later described the encounter on his Facebook page: 'On a personal note, this was the first time I've ever spoken with a world leader entirely in a foreign language. I consider that a meaningful personal milestone. It was an honour to meet President Xi and other leaders.' In March 2016, on a visit to the Chinese capital, Zuckerberg met with Jack Ma as well as Liu Yunshan, head of propaganda and one of the seven members of the Politburo Standing Committee, the very heart of power in China. But '[e]ven if Facebook were to make it in the Chinese market, at what cost would it come, not only in cash but in reputation?' asks Lincoln Davidson, research associate at the Council on Foreign Relations, in a post on the US think-tank's blog. 'Any time there's been even the slightest suggestion that American companies are involved in Chinese censorship efforts, they've been widely derided in the press.'

Obstructing foreign economic actors is actually quite easy—they just need to be asked to accept censorship. This is not just a defensive tactic; the Chinese powers have grasped the importance of soft power. Xi encourages official media outlets to spread the good word abroad, in English. Twitter and Facebook may be inaccessible in China, but Beijing still uses them outside its borders to spread its propaganda. There is also a surprising level of co-operation between Beijing and Hollywood, under the aegis of businessmen close to the regime, such as Wang Jianlin, in the production of 'blockbusters with Chinese characteristics'. Access to the Chinese market is so appealing that the American industry is ready to make certain compromises, to such a degree that some congressmen have expressed concern: the issue of studio acquisition, for instance, was brought before the US administration. In October 2016, *The Washington Post* warned its readers: 'It is not far-fetched to assume that China would seek to spread pro-regime propaganda via ownership of U.S. entertainment media.'

Since the aim is to control minds and souls, ideology and culture are on the frontline of Xi's war. He underlined this in an August 2013 speech to the National Propaganda and Ideology Work Conference in Beijing: 'Economic construction is the Party's central work, and ideological work is extremely important work of the Party'. To accomplish this work efficiently, of course, one must be well-trained. This means going back to basics: Mao's teachings must be known inside-out. Marxist-Leninist teachings were a priority issue for Xi's first presidential term.

> Party members and cadres must have firm Marxist and communist beliefs ... Leading cadres and especially high-level cadres must systematically grasp basic Marxist theory as their special skill, be honest and conscientious, and study Marxism-Leninism, Mao Zedong Thought and especially Deng Xiaoping Theory, the important 'Three Represents' thought and the scientific development view from beginning to end. Party schools, cadre academies, academies of social science, higher education institutes, theoretical study centres, etc., must all make the study of Marxism mandatory, and become important battlegrounds for Marxist study, research, and propaganda. New cadres and young cadres must especially grasp theoretical study ... master the use of Marxist positions, viewpoints and methods to examine and resolve problems.

The joys of theory!

In 2014, the Academy of Social Sciences—the Beijing-based national research body employing thousands of researchers—was issued a warning following an inspection by the Party's Central Commission for Discipline Inspection. Invited to a study session on the ideas of Xi Jinping, the inspector found that the Academy had 'ideological problems' and had been 'infiltrated by foreign forces'. The message was received, loud and clear; measures have since been taken. In 2015 and 2016, the Academy published no fewer than four critical works on 'historical nihilism', 'neoliberalism', the 'theory of universal values', and the 'concept of Western constitutional democracy'. The last three shared the same preface; here are a few excerpts to gauge the country's mood:

> Facing a new situation wherein our cultural ideology is undergoing a process of exchange, blending, and confrontation, the paramount task facing the frontlines of philosophical social science is not only to persist in upholding Marxism as our guiding ideology, but to engage in meaningful critiques of 'universal values', the concept of 'constitutional democracy', neoliberalism, historical nihilism, democratic socialism, and other mistaken ideologies from this position. We must place unfailing faith in the path of 'Socialism with Chinese characteristics', matched with an equal degree of faith in our theories, and faith in our systems.

The Academy followed the roadmap outlined in Document 9 to the letter. An entitled form of Marxism is expressed here, eager to lambast its opponents: Westerners used their universal values to impose their law all over the world—in Afghanistan, Iraq, Syria, Libya and Yemen—but

> What is clear is that what the system of Western capitalist values brought to these countries was not the 'gospel' or 'salvation'" but instead unmitigated unrest and disaster. The cruel lesson learned by these countries and regions demonstrates that there is no such thing as eternal values which can be universally applied to all societies, all countries, and all peoples.

On the contrary, the preface continues, there is discernibly

> an ideological trap, aimed at our nation, with the goal of destroying the status of Marxism and replacing it with the ideology of the Western bourgeoisie. ... Our nation is a socialist nation with a specific history and unique realities. What system or methods are appropriate for our nation should be decided by the national circumstances of our nation. Simply copying the political system or political methods of another country would be pointless, and might even have dire consequences for the future of our nation. China is a socialist nation and a developing superpower. We must make use of the beneficial aspects of foreign political civilisations, but never at the cost of abandoning the fundamental political system of 'Socialism with Chinese characteristics'.

This passage could have been written, word for word, years before: it is pure, hard ideology. On an economic level, the United States' sub-prime crisis of 2008, which led to the global financial crisis, is described here as 'the complete bankruptcy of neoliberalism':

> It demonstrates that contemporary capitalism has not fundamentally solved the inherent contradiction which exists between socialised and private production. Periodic economic crises are an unavoidable product of this fundamental contradiction of capitalism. It is precisely because socialist market economics employs a different model, wherein the means of production are held communally, that economic crises are not only avoidable, but also predictable.

Universities have also been called upon to lead the charge. On campus, Marx is firmly back in fashion. One of Beijing's two great universities, Beida, has launched 'six Marx projects'. One of these involves the erection of an edifice replicating aspects of the 'red building', where Mao and the first Revolutionaries worked. In October 2015, the university organised the first World Congress on Marxism, a sort of 'Marxist Davos' to be held every two years. Foreign guests included many old-timers, like Samir Amin, the Franco-Egyptian economist and anti-globalisation theorist. Beida also wants to assemble a large library collection of Marxist texts, similar to those it holds on Confucianism, Buddhism, and Taoism, aimed at shaping the 'new generation of experts'. 'The documentary centre of research pertaining to Marxism should be in China, and on the campus of Peking University,' explained Sun Daiyao, dean of the university's School of Marxism.

Mobilisation for this culture war has been widespread, and artists have also been enlisted: Xi reminded them of this in October 2014 during the forum on literature and art in Beijing. Artists of all ages and all disciplines—writers, actors, directors, screenwriters, dancers—gathered at the Great Hall of the People in the capital, to talk with the president. Among them was Mo Yan, who had been awarded the Nobel Prize for Literature two years before, a source of great national pride; he paid special heed to Xi's words. Also present were two great filmmakers: Chen Kaige, the director of *Farewell My Concubine*, and Feng Xiaogang, who specialises in Chinese New Year blockbusters.

One of the participants, Tie Ning, chairwoman of the China Writers Association, stated that 'when I heard about the forum, I was not in Beijing. On my way back to China, I could not help but think of the Yan'an Forum on literature and art seventy-two years ago.' While for her this was a positive association, to intellectual liberals it is a chilling parallel. During the forum of May 1942, Mao had firmly reminded writers and artists of their duty to serve the Party, and that their 'fundamental task' was to become the 'loyal spokespersons of the masses'. In the name of China's liberation, Mao fought on not only 'the front of the gun', but also the 'front of the pen'—the intellectual front. A rectification movement had followed his speech; those who had dared criticise the Party leaders' privileges were tracked down. The young writer Wang Shiwei was one of them—he was imprisoned, accused of being a Guomindang spy, and executed. Seven decades later, there is no need for such violent means; times have changed. All the same, Xi Jinping believes artists should be told that it's time to become politically involved, and that they must contribute to the revival of the 'Chinese dream': 'To realise the Great Rejuvenation of the Chinese nation Chinese culture must flourish. Our modern art and literature needs to take patriotism as its muse.'

The mood at the forum was relaxed, but Xi's tone was firm. Casting himself as the arbiter of socialist good taste, he warned that, in recent years, problems had arisen:

> Since the reforms and opening up, China's literary and artistic creation has ushered in a new springtime and produced a large number of outstanding works. At the same time, it cannot be denied that in terms of literary and artistic creation, there is also a lack of quality, problems of plagiarism and imitation, stereotyping, and problems of mechanised production and rapid consumption. Some works are lofty and distort the classics, subvert history, vilify the people and heroes; some do not distinguish between true or false, do not discriminate between good and evil, and make ugliness beautiful, over-emphasising the dark side of society; some are

bizarre, vulgar and low-level, they regard the work as a 'cash cow'.

Such artists, Xi said, were out of touch with 'the people and reality', and 'all this warns us that literature and art cannot be lost in the tide of the market economy'. Showing a sudden awareness of the noble futility of art, he added: 'I talked with several artists and asked what the most prominent issue with current literature and art was. They invariably all replied: impulsiveness. Some think that it is not worthwhile to repeatedly polish a work that cannot be finished in a timely manner and converted to a practical value, or, in time, into yuan.' This was a jibe at artists who cater to Western tastes, making a fortune in New York or London.

Xi stressed that the Chinese artist's main concern must be the people of China: 'The people are not abstract concepts'. He gave the example of Liu Qing (1916–78), a writer from Shaanxi province known for his novel *The Builders*, an epic narrative of the lives of peasants after the Communists' victory:

In 1952, Liu Qing served as deputy secretary of the county Party Committee of Chang'an County, Shaanxi. He later resigned from the position of deputy secretary of the county party committee and retained the post of standing committee member, and settled there in the village of Huangfu, where he spent fourteen years and concentrated on creating *The Builders*. Because he had a deep understanding of peasant life in

Guanzhong, Shaanxi, the characters he depicted were lifelike. He was familiar with the joys and sorrows of the peasants. Whenever the Central Government introduced a policy involving rural peasants, he immediately knew whether the peasants would be happy or unhappy.

Under Xi, not only are artists required to be close to the people, but they are also supposed to draw on the 'magnificent traditional culture' which he sets against 'the agitated world culture' of today: 'Enhancing cultural awareness and cultural self-confidence is the way to reach self-confidence: confidence in our theories, and confidence in our system.' He even used a Hollywood reference to support his argument:

> Foreigners run to us to search for material and find inspiration. Were not Hollywood films such as *Kung Fu Panda* and *Mulan* based on our cultural resources? ... Inheriting Chinese culture is not a simple retrospective practice, nor is it blind xenophobia; rather, it is the past serving the present, using the foreign for Chinese purposes, dialectics, innovation; abandoning negative factors, and inheriting positive thinking.

Xi is a great proponent of 'positive energy' (*zhengnengliang*): 'as long as there is positive energy and infectious power that can warm the soul and enlighten the mind, it will be an outstanding work of art.' A few weeks after the forum, *The People's Daily* invoked the newly fashionable 'positive energy' to express its concern over the trend among young people of flaunting their 'loser' status (*diaosi*, literally 'dick hair'). 'Many young people nowadays call themselves losers ... Whether male or female, whether moderately successful or sluggishly decadent, everyone is either consciously or subconsciously striving for this label. If you don't claim it,' the newspaper explained disapprovingly, 'it's as if you're alienated from the masses'. Originating online, *diaosi* was at first used pejoratively to describe losers or failures—all those who had failed to find their place in successful China. But it has now been reclaimed by an increasing number of young people who have rejected the system and its wealth-seeking culture, or who despise the heirs of the communist regime and their exorbitant privileges. A counter-culture has been born. To be a *diaosi* is no longer an insult, but a badge of honour. Media and marketing have started using it. One comedian even dined out on it with a series criticising the flaws of urban China, broadcast on Sohu, one of the biggest websites in the country.

But Xi Jinping fails to see the irony. At the 2014 literature and art forum, he honoured two young bloggers, devoid of evil spirit, who celebrate 'positive energy'. One of them, a man in his thirties, Zhou Xiaoping, became known thanks to his attacks on the United States; Xi encouraged him to continue his 'work of positive energy'. On social media, the loser army quickly retaliated against Zhou, calling him the '50 Cent King' in reference to the sum the regime pays bloggers to post 'positive' comments. In any case, Zhou has joined the cohort of boot-lickers, or *paimapi*—those who pat the horse's backside, to employ the Chinese expression for sycophants.

They are many. Some commentators, noting the extent to which such reverence is organised, see it as a revival of the personality cult, which Deng Xiaoping had been sure to ban in the 1980s. This return to the past fits neatly into the current celebrity era, thanks to the *mise en scène* of the presidential couple, which fully corresponds with today's norms: Xi is married to a popular singer, the star of Chinese New Year television galas. The couple, both in their fifties, are rather dashing. The propaganda machine occasionally nicknames them 'Uncle Xi' or 'Mama Peng', as if they were two sympathetic cartoon characters. At such moments, Xi seems a far cry from the number-one enemy of dissidents, human rights lawyers and NGOs.

In this fairy tale 2.0, narrated by numerous videos and songs broadcast on social media, the presidential couple, like latter-day Kennedys, are benevolent towards the people and welcomed with enthusiasm all over the world. Emerging from their plane, Xi Jinping and the elegant Peng Liyuan are always smiling and radiant. If all the women in the country dream of marrying Uncle Xi, it is said, his love is for Mrs Peng alone. As in the Mao days, when even Mao's personal life was glorified, a group of musicians from Henan province wrote a song along these lines, broadcast on social media. Entitled *Xi Dada Loves Peng Mama*, it is a pop ballad similar to those heard on buses and in karaoke bars. The lyrics are kitsch and syrupy. Here is a short excerpt:

Xi Dada loves Peng Mama,
This sort of love is legendary,
Peng Mama loves Xi Dada,
A nation with love is the strongest!

Xi Dada loves Peng Mama
When they are together, he always smiles at her happily
Peng Mama loves Xi Dada
Holding his hand, her smile is a beautiful flower

Undoubtedly, Xi's neo-authoritarianism can be described as dictatorship, celebrity-style.

9

SHEDDING THE LOW PROFILE

There was once a rare moment of truth when Xi Jinping, usually so in control of his public persona, came out of his shell. Particularly, he emerged from the shell of cunning cautiousness that generally characterises speeches given abroad by leaders of the Chinese Communist Party. Xi was in Mexico, the 'backyard' of China's great American rival. In February 2009, he was already one of the favourites for the leadership, but was still only vice-president. He was shoring up his international standing with multiple trips abroad. Standing confidently behind the microphone in front of the Chinese embassy in Mexico, he faced a specially-selected audience of compatriots—expats, diplomats, businessmen, and students. The peaceful atmosphere made his remarks all the more striking: 'There are certain well-fed foreigners who have nothing better to do than point the finger,' Xi declared. 'Yet, firstly, China is not exporting revolution, secondly, we are not the ones exporting poverty or famine either, thirdly, we do not cause problems in other people's countries. What more can I say?'

It went without saying that those who did export famine and unrest were obviously the Americans. For the deputy chief of mission at the US Embassy in Mexico, there could be no mistaking this, as he pointed out in a diplomatic telegram, describing Xi's 'unusual behaviour', 'which contrasts strongly with the theme of global cooperation' promoted at the start of his visit 'to a country with strong ties to the United States.' China is particularly resentful of being a target for Western criticism when it deems its American rival to be a much more questionable world superpower. Xi's declaration was manifesting real annoyance. It is usually his wont, when abroad, to evoke the pacific rise of his country and 'win-win' agreements. This sudden rage revealed to all the new-found national pride permeating the Party's leadership and clamouring to be heard: China, now endowed with a strong economy and army, no longer needed lessons from anyone. Beware, it said: China has become touchy.

The 1990s were probably the tipping point when a well-studied modesty gave way to demonstrations of national pride. In 1996, an overtly nationalist book, *China Can Say No*, became a bestseller. Written by five young intellectuals, the book accuses the United States of hindering China's growth and wanting to 'contain' it as Washington had done with the Soviet Union during the Cold War. In 2009, some of these authors struck again with another work, *Unhappy China*, asserting that the country must adopt a hegemonic position in the world from which to oppose Western influence. The time had come to take a leading international role. Far from pulling back, what was needed was an expansion of influence. In a blend of cultural patriotism and political messianism, one of the book's authors, Huang Jisu, explained to a Chinese newspaper:

> If it wants to feature among the leaders of the world, China must absolutely equip itself with superior assets ... It must not lose the achievement of five thousand years of history. We need to reclaim a large part of what we have shunned ... Not only must China save itself, but it must also save humanity ... The Chinese people must shoulder this task, no matter how heavy.

The *fenqing* ('angry youth') ensured the book was a success—the term describes young nationalists, urban dwellers active on social media and the wider internet, who know how to make themselves heard in the public arena and are looked upon favourably by the government. One year earlier at the time of the Beijing Olympics, and under the indulgent eye of the government, they had launched the campaign to boycott the French supermarket chain Carrefour, following the incidents that had affected the Olympic torch relay in Paris. One month later, they had spontaneously gone to Sichuan province to take part in rescue operations after a violent earthquake in which more than 70,000 had died.

At that time, I joined a small group of students in the mountains near Chengdu. Over the course of the day, they gradually and symptomatically revealed themselves to be critical of the fact that I was a French journalist. One gave me a straight-faced warning, inspired by the Liverpool anthem: 'We'll never walk alone'. We, he told me, are a force to be reckoned with; we are to be feared and we know it. It was on this surge of national pride that Xi rode as soon as he came to power. He would flatter these young nationalists on the one hand, and on the other would reach out to the proponents of 1980s neo-authoritarianism, who were persuaded that only a strong regime had been able to save the country after the repression of the Tiananmen movement. Gone were the days when, following the 1989 massacre, China had been marginalised by other nations and Deng advised 'keeping a low profile and biding our time' (*taoguang yanghui*, 'hide from brightness and nourish obscurity'). This counsel of reserve summarised the strategy Deng had formulated in twenty-eight characters in an address to future generations: 'Observe calmly; secure our position; cope with affairs calmly; hide our capacities and bide our time; be good at maintaining a low profile; and never claim leadership'.

Xi has broken with this low-profile doctrine, giving encouragement to young and not-so-young generations of nationalists—even, as we have seen, if this means reviving the old enmity with Japan. Even if it involves explicitly identifying the United States as the great twenty-first-century enemy, always presented as being determined to weaken China. With conspiracy theory lending a hand, this version of reality has found many takers.

In 2013, a documentary produced by the People's Liberation Army, entitled *Silent Contest*, caused a great stir. It argued that, since the fall of the Soviet Union, Beijing had become the Americans' enemy number one. To achieve its ends, the United States had embarked on an 'ideological war', much more efficient than a traditional war. As Li Zhiye, president of the China Institute of Contemporary International Relations, explained in the film: 'Since the Vietnam war, the US has more often chosen the strategy of "winning without a war." This is a soft war using politics, economics, ideas, and culture as weapons with its advantageous military power as backing.' *Silent Contest* generally develops the same ideas as Document 9: that the Americans support NGOs who seek to overthrow the Party, and seek to bribe Chinese soldiers or influence Chinese young people with their 'vulgar' culture, using social media and other online platforms. Much as the Arab uprisings would be treated two years later, the unrest in Iran in 2009 is given as an example of the Americans' capacity to influence the young. The film was banned a few weeks after its release, and there is no way of knowing if the reason was the nature of its content, perhaps deemed to be overly explicit.

It is against this American soft power that the nationalist discourse calls for China to fight, with varying degrees of prudence. Nevertheless, this does not mean that Xi has neglected the classic military route. His predecessors had already embarked on the modernisation of the army and increased the military's budget, the second largest in the world after the United States. Xi went even further, using the fight against corruption to launch sweeping reform. It was the perfect excuse to make some heads roll and appoint his own men. Xi prides himself on his military knowledge. He readily draws attention to the fact that, in the early 1980s, he was the personal assistant (*mishu*) of the then minister of national defence, Geng Biao. In 2016, Xi suddenly gave himself a new title, that of Commander-in-Chief. He is now in charge of everyday operations in case of external conflicts or regional tensions.

Such tensions have become more frequent and more acute during Xi's time in office. Mathieu Duchâtel, a specialist on the Chinese army and director of the Asia programme at the European Council on Foreign Relations, explains: 'What sets Xi apart from his predecessors is his tendency to use the military tool, not for engaging in military actions, but for conducting his foreign policy.' This was first seen in the East China Sea, around the inhabited islands of Senkaku, which are under Tokyo's jurisdiction but claimed by Beijing and known there as Diaoyu. In 2013 Xi multiplied naval and aerial incursions and set up an air defence identification zone, placing the islands de facto under his sovereignty. Meanwhile, timely anti-Japanese protests broke out in several towns in the country.

Xi has made the same assertion of power in the South China Sea, ordering that artificial islands be built to manifest Chinese presence in territories over which neighbouring countries such as Vietnam and the Philippines claim sovereignty. With this move, Beijing has, for the first time, flouted a ruling of the intergovernmental Permanent Court of Arbitration in The Hague. In the summer of 2016, following an appeal from Manila, the Court concluded that Beijing had 'violated the Philippines's sovereign rights'. Yet Xi clearly rejected the ruling at a July summit with EU leaders: 'Our national sovereignty and our maritime rights and interests in the South China Sea will not be affected in any way by the ruling and case brought about by the Philippines.' The Xinhua state news agency was even more explicit in a statement published soon after the Court's pronouncement, denouncing a Western plot to contain China's development. It quoted the Chinese ambassador in the Netherlands, Wu Ken, who predicted that the day of the ruling would be remembered in history as a 'black Tuesday for The Hague', and asserted that the decision 'dishonoured international law'.

Xi's line of attack—or from his viewpoint, his means of establishing himself—has included making the most of Western countries' weakness after the financial crisis of 2008. As Mao said, one must seize the moment. In the same period, intellectuals started to demand their country's 'right to speak' (*huayuquan*) and defended the existence of a 'Chinese model' (*Zhongguo moshi*). In 2009, Liu Yang, one the authors of *China Can Say No* and *Unhappy China*, published *China Has No Model* in the same vein. The book's subtitle leaves no doubt as to its tone: *The West Has No God, the United States are not Saviours*. Liu argued that China must now find its own path. In order to do so, it must re-engage with its traditional philosophy, and in particular with Confucian morals and ethics, the opposites of capitalist interests. Indeed, the prosperity brought about by Deng Xiaoping's reform policy had led to issues of corruption and social inequality, but had also allowed China to rediscover its strength. Above all, it had convinced the majority of the Chinese people that Western culture was unsuitable for their country. Four years before Xi came to power, Liu was already evoking the 'Chinese Dream', which must 'be extensive and belong to all of humanity'. He predicted that 'one day, in the future, the world will be thankful for China's existence.'

Has Xi read Liu Yang's work? Probably. Like Liu, he maintains a positive way of speaking about the culture and exceptionalism of China, whose ancestral treasures justify the country's embarking on a path towards its own special kind of policy. If China is not Europe, why should it be a democracy, a system born in a world so far removed from China? In his speech on art and literature in October 2014, reminiscent of Mao's 1942 speech, Xi referred to the German philosopher Karl Jaspers (1883–1969) and his 'axial age' concept, which was popular in the 1950s but had since become obsolete: the idea that the world had known a period, similar to a dawn of civilisation, when powerful cultures had emerged all over the world. Xi described it thus:

> The German philosopher Jaspers wrote in the book *The Origin and Goal of History* that from 800 BCE to 200 BCE was the 'axial age' of human civilisation and a major breakthrough in human civilisation. Ancient Greece, ancient China, ancient India, and other civilisations all produced great thinkers. The ideological principles they proposed shaped different cultural traditions and have always influenced human life.

He added, 'These words are very profound and insightful. Throughout the ages, the reason why the Chinese nation has had status and influence in the world is not because it relied on militarism, nor external expansion, but because of the powerful appeal and attraction of Chinese culture.' In developing this concept, Jaspers had tried to find a possible unity in global humanity. Xi, on the other hand, saw in it a subtle means of presenting China as a civilisation apart, to justify its unique development. In another speech, before a gathering of members of the Chinese diaspora in Beijing, he insisted on the importance of the ties to the nation: 'The five thousand years of Chinese civilisation are an intellectual strength ... No matter where they find themselves, Chinese citizens carry the distinctive markers of their culture and this is the spiritual gene shared by all Chinese people.' The 'spiritual gene' is rather an enigmatic notion, but the common ground of humanity in Jaspers' original work has clearly given way here to an exclusive conception of civilisation, impermeable to cultural mixing and outside influences.

Of course, Xi does not come up with these ideas all by himself. Since the 2008 crisis, numerous works on the 'Chinese model' have been published. Another bestseller of interest to us, written by Professor Zhang Weiwei of Fudan University, Shanghai, is *The China Wave: Rise of a Civilizational State*—apparently recommended by Xi himself to Robert Zoellick, former president of the World Bank. Zhang claims that to impose a Western model on an old civilisation—in other words, to impose reforms that may lead to democracy—is a heresy. 'If a civilizational state like China follows the Western model, the country will experience chaos and break up. Indeed, in retrospect, if China had followed the Western model rather than adhering to its own path, the country could have disintegrated just like the Soviet Union and Yugoslavia.' Similar to Samuel Huntington and his theses on the clash of civilisations—Western, Islamic, Hindu, Orthodox, Japanese, African, Latin American, and Sinic

[Chinese]—Zhang believes that China as a civilisational state is self-sufficient: 'Sun Tzu's *The Art of War* does not need the approval of Clausewitz, Confucius does not need the acknowledgment of Plato, and China's current "macroeconomic regulation" does not need the approval of the US Federal Reserve Board.' On the contrary, Zhang, like many of his colleagues, argues that China will be the one to influence the world. For him, we are moving away from a vertical world with the West at the top, to a horizontal world where all countries, including China, will be equal to the West, in terms of both wealth and ideas. 'This is an unprecedented shift of economic and political gravity in human history, which will change the world forever.'

The good news, according to Zhang, is that Xi Jinping will be the man implementing this new paradigm. 'He is a confident leader who is ready to share the Chinese experience with his counterparts all over the world,' he explains. 'Many countries now turn to China for inspiration, for it has been far more successful than many others over the past forty years, in particular when dealing with issues such as eradicating poverty and the emergence of the largest middle class in the world.'

In face of the challenges of globalisation, then, it is not a question of a 'Chinese model', but of the 'Chinese solution' (*Zhongguo fang'an*). Xi used the expression for the first time in July 2016, in a speech marking the ninety-fifth anniversary of the Chinese Communist Party.

The whole Party must remember that what we are building is 'Socialism with Chinese characteristics', not some other–ism. History has not ended, nor can it possibly end. To judge 'Socialism with Chinese characteristics' we must look to fact, and to the judgment of the Chinese people, and not to the subjective and groundless conclusions of biased people. The [Party] and Chinese people have every confidence in their ability to provide a Chinese solution to aid the search for a better social system for humanity.

China now has the 'solution', which it readily shares. Conveniently, the Western model is running out of steam, and not just because of the 2008 financial crisis. Democratic fatigue is spreading. Europe is facing difficulties, is worn out by Brexit, and has no plan. Inequalities are rising in the rich world and the 'losers' of globalisation are ready to vote for parties that promise a strong state. In the United States, the election of Donald Trump caused widespread astonishment and showed how unpredictable democracy can be. The Chinese media gladly seized this perfect opportunity to tell the story of an election that revealed American democracy's flaws. In October 2016, *The People's Daily* claimed that the 'U.S. presidential election chaos exposes a flawed political system'. Ramming the point home, it even presumed to lecture the Americans, counselling them to 'take a close, honest look at [their] arrogant democracy'.

For many years now, the Chinese state has responded to Washington's annual report on human rights in China with its own counter-report. In these rebuttals, the State Council (government)'s Information Office scrupulously outlines all of its rival's flaws: growing insecurity, a rise in gun crime, increasing racial discrimination and economic inequalities—all of which invalidate the United States' claim to be the land of the free. The 2016 counter-report, made public the following year, gleefully pointed out that American politics had 'recently'—presumably since Trump came to power—given further cause to believe that its elections were a 'farce dominated by money politics'. As for the presidential campaign itself, it had been full of 'lies'. And the people had responded with 'with waves of boycotts and protests, giving full exposure to the hypocritical nature of U.S. democracy'.

The notion that the global democratic system has many faults is gaining ground, and, luckily for Beijing, it is increasingly easy to convince the masses of it. Xi is not the only one on the international stage promoting an alternative model, and this is certainly a development of the twenty-first century. Xi's solution strongly resembles the authoritarian propositions of Russia's Vladimir Putin, Hungary's Viktor Orbán, and Turkey's Recep Tayyip Erdoğan. Are we now hearing the opening bars of an illiberal *Internationale*? In a 2014 speech, Prime Minister Orbán emphasised that the defining aspect of today's world can be articulated as a race to figure out a way of organising communities, a state that is most capable of making a nation competitive. This is why ... a trending topic in [current] thinking is understanding systems that are not Western, not liberal, not liberal democracies, maybe not even democracies, and yet making nations successful. Today, the stars of international analyses are Singapore, China, India, Turkey, Russia.

If Rome is no longer in Rome and Europe tolerates the emergence in its midst of autocratic experiments, then there is nothing to hinder the expansion of the Chinese model. China can present itself as a positive and credible world power. Isn't the proof of China's efficiency—and its particular benevolence towards Europe—in the Belt and Road Initiative, the new terrestrial and maritime Silk Road project launched by Xi in 2013 with a colossal investment of $1,000 billion?

In the space of a few years, under Xi, China has greatly increased its presence in Central and Eastern Europe, making the most of the European Union's apathy. The Balkans, an important crossroads between Asia and Europe, are the target of choice: in 2014, Beijing promised a $3 billion investment fund, a year after offering a credit line of $10 billion. Vuk Vuksanovic, a researcher and former Serbian diplomat, explained the strategy in 2017: 'While Westerners have generally viewed the Balkan region as a nuisance—an ethnically fragmented territory on the periphery of the Euro-Atlantic world— China thinks of the Balkans as a conduit to European markets, as well as a way to project its soft power and buy friends among new E.U. members and potential membership candidates.'

It seems that Xi is saying, 'Yes, we can'. China is sure of itself; the 'Chinese Dream' also includes the ability to attract allies thanks to its financial power, evidenced by the creation of the Asian Infrastructure Investment Bank in early 2016. China now prides itself on being the only world power able to stand up to the United States, culturally, economically, and militarily. This global leadership has shown itself in unlikely areas: civil servants from non-democratic African or South-East Asian countries, for instance, are sent to Beijing for propaganda training.

Further evidence of the success of Chinese soft power could be seen in the first couple's visit to the United States in April 2017. They were invited to Donald Trump's residence in Mar-a-Lago, Florida, where the American president's young granddaughter performed a Chinese song. Her parents were proud to show off her progress in Mandarin. This scene, innocent as it may then have seemed, could soon become the symbol of a geopolitical turn.

In any case, after having targeted China during his presidential campaign—'We can't continue to allow China to rape our country, and that's what they're doing.

It's the greatest theft in the history of the world,' he declared in May 2016—President Trump eventually had a change of heart. His first encounter with Xi Jinping did not turn out to be the violent clash he had predicted. On the contrary, Trump was full of praise in an interview with *The Wall Street Journal*: 'We have a great chemistry together. We like each other. I like him a lot. I think his wife is terrific.' Xi had even been so bold as to give Trump a brief history lesson on Chinese–North Korean relations. 'After listening for 10 minutes, I realized it's not so easy,' Trump admitted.

Is Donald Trump nothing more than a 'paper tiger', who will let Xi Jinping lay out his pieces on the board, like the avid Go player he is? Xi's Go partner and childhood friend is none other than Nie Weiping, a professional player who became a national hero in the 1980s after multiple victories against the Japanese champion. Will the US president let himself be 'surrounded' by such a lover of the ancient strategy game? Xi would do well to beware of Trump's volatility. Tensions remain, in particular regarding the status of Taiwan; they constantly give rise to rumours, and not all of them are entirely nebulous. In the summer of 2016, a report by the Rand Corporation, a respected think-tank close to US military circles, noted that war was improbable, but not implausible:

> China and the United States are at loggerheads over several regional disputes that could lead to military

confrontation or even violence between them. Both countries have large concentrations of military forces operating in close proximity. If an incident occurred or a crisis overheated, both have an incentive to strike enemy forces before being struck by them. And if hostilities erupted, both have ample forces, technology, industrial might, and personnel to fight across vast expanses of land, sea, air, space, and cyberspace.

A Harvard political scientist, Graham Allison, has coined the phrase 'Thucydides Trap', named for the ancient Greek historian. According to Thucydides, war broke out between Sparta and Athens because the Spartans were concerned about the emergence of Athens as a power. Can Washington and Beijing avoid the same fate? Allison, who turned this geopolitical question into a research project, promoted the concept so well that Xi himself referred to it in front of his Western hosts in November 2013: 'We must work together to avoid the Thucydides Trap'.

Since then, Donald Trump has come to power in the United States, aiming to 'make America great again'. In his speech of 18 December 2017, in which he presented his national security strategy, Trump identified China as one of the 'rival powers' who 'challenge American power, influence, and interests, attempting to erode American security and prosperity'. But he also argued in the same speech that strategic cooperation between the two countries should continue. Will these two nationalists manage to avoid confrontation and develop a harmonious and peaceful coexistence? World peace depends on their ability to get along.

10

'XI-ISM'

Is there such a thing as 'Xi-ism'? Perhaps something similar to Maoism—that sinified version of Marxism-Leninism that once appealed to so many Western youths? This is an important question in China and is heavily discussed within academic circles. It is all the more interesting since each leader leaves his mark, a sort of theoretical legacy, in the Constitution and Party statutes. This comes in the form of a personal slogan, which serves as a summary of the leader's political objectives and is repeated like a mantra and reprised by his successors. The Xi 'magic formula' adopted by the Nineteenth Congress in autumn 2017 was 'Xi Jinping Thought on Socialism with Chinese Characteristics for a New Era.'

First of all, it is worth noting that Xi has managed the incredible feat of having his name inscribed in the Party constitution, putting himself on the same level as Mao alone—'Mao Zedong Thought' was added in 1945 at the Eighth Congress. Even Deng's 'Socialism with

Chinese characteristics' was not added until after his death, adopted by the Fifteenth Congress as 'Deng Xiaoping Theory' in 1997. Xi, then, has been given *lingxiu* status, a term which means 'leader' in Chinese, but which up until that point had been reserved for Mao and Deng.

The 'Xi Jinping Thought' formula announced the start of a new thirty-year era, ending in 2050, following those of Maoism and of Deng and his heirs, Jiang and Hu. Xi has asserted himself as an all-powerful master and guide. He is to lead China down the path of a two-stage development to become 'a great modern socialist country': between 2020 and 2035, the aim is to achieve a 'moderately prosperous society', the Confucian expression used by Deng; then, between 2035 and 2050, the Chinese nation will once again be a leading world economy. It will be 'prosperous, strong, democratic, culturally advanced, harmonious, and beautiful,' Xi declared to 2,200 delegates. Democratic, that is, in the Party's sense of the word, of course, and not that of despised Western norms. The good Marxist Xi also pointed out that 'the principal contradiction' facing Chinese society was between 'unbalanced and inadequate development and the people's ever-growing needs for a better life.'

For Xi, this new era—his era—will be that of a fully-assumed rejuvenation. About time, one might say. The late-nineteenth-century reformers had dreamed of it, the Party will fulfil it: 'The Chinese nation, with an entirely new posture, now stands tall and firm in the East,' he declared. To get to this point, Xi had put the Party back at the heart of things, to control society and the economy and achieve the 'Chinese Dream'. He announced with pride: 'National rejuvenation has been the greatest dream of the Chinese people since modern times began. At its founding, the Communist Party of China made realising communism its highest ideal and its ultimate goal, and shouldered the historic mission of national rejuvenation. In pursuing this goal, the Party has united the Chinese people and led them through arduous struggles to epic accomplishments'.

When it comes down to it, on which side does Xi Jinping fall in the battle of ideas? He is neither entirely on the right, which defends constitutional evolution, nor entirely on the left, where the authoritarian Maoist nostalgics are gathered. Like all politicians, he manoeuvres, tinkers, and seeks his balance, giving his encouragement here and there. There is no indication that he is the author of a coherent doctrine of his own.

Everyone has their own take on this matter, and the dissident writer Murong Xuecun sees in these trends the rise of a 'new market totalitarianism', a totalitarianism adapted to the twenty-first century. Thus, where Hu Jintao was overwhelmed by social media, Xi Jinping can force social networks into line and impose his law on digital spaces. He even uses tweets and Facebook posts himself. The personality cult, back with a vengeance, has had to resort to the codes of trendy youth. 'The people are granted some personal freedoms,' Murong explains, 'but everyone is aware that these can be revoked at any time and without warning.' Despite this acclimatisation to the digital environment, he predicts that the regime will fall 'by 2035'. 'This system of social "harmonisation" has reached its limit, and many people expect another Tiananmen, like in 1989.'

Indeed, this is the final and most important question: is Xi's China stable? Of course, it is vain to speculate on the country's future, and no one can say whether the regime will fall all at once or if its leaders are devising a new enviable, solid, and competitive—anything but democratic—model. It is important to note, however, that sinologists have become increasingly sceptical since 2015. Until then, opinions had diverged. Some believed that, since 1949, the Party had demonstrated its ability to adapt to different circumstances, in some sense the world's first 'Darwinian' Leninist Party. Others constantly predicted the fall of the regime due to economic vulnerabilities and social tensions, echoing Gordon Chang's opinion—he had become the object of ridicule in 2001 for authoring a book in which he predicted the fall of the communist system by 2011.

By contrast, few today believe the regime will survive. A penny appears to have dropped among the world's China experts: the American sinologist David Shambaugh, who had been confident of Beijing's strength until 2015, and whose position was well-known, joined the ranks of the sceptics. In an extremely critical article published in *The Wall Street Journal*, he predicted an imminent end to the regime. The latter, he argued, was down to its last cards:

> The endgame of Chinese communist rule ... has progressed further than many think. We don't know what the pathway from now until the end will look like, of course. It will probably be highly unstable and unsettled. But until the system begins to unravel in some obvious way, those inside of it will play along—thus contributing to the facade of stability. Communist rule in China is unlikely to end quietly. A single event is unlikely to trigger a peaceful implosion of the regime. Its demise is likely to be protracted, messy and violent. I wouldn't rule out the possibility that Mr. Xi will be deposed in a power struggle or coup d'état. With his aggressive anticorruption campaign ... he is overplaying a weak hand and deeply aggravating key party, state, military and commercial constituencies.

To stress his point, Shambaugh identified several signs of weakness: flight of the rich from the country, political repression, lack of faith in the system among many of its followers, an exhausted economy, and corruption, an evil which, without the rule of law and with the media under the regime's thumb, is deeply entrenched. Shambaugh referred to a personal experience, a conference in Beijing on the 'Chinese Dream' organised by a Party-affiliated think-tank:

We sat through two days of mind-numbing, non-stop presentations by two dozen party scholars—but their faces were frozen, their body language was wooden, and their boredom was palpable. They feigned compliance with the party and their leader's latest mantra. But it was evident that the propaganda had lost its power, and the emperor had no clothes.

To save the system would take reform, Shambaugh asserted, but Xi has not come around to it. Thus, he concluded: 'We cannot predict when Chinese communism will collapse, but it is hard not to conclude that we are witnessing its final phase. The CCP is the world's second-longest ruling regime (behind only North Korea), and no party can rule forever.'

To quote another eminent China specialist, Jean-Pierre Cabestan, 'barring any interior or international catastrophe, it is highly probably that the current regime will stay in power and ensure the stability of the country, at least for the next five to ten years. No-one can say what China's political future holds after that.'

So, will Xi Jinping win his bet? Will he ensure that the Party keeps pace with a society in motion? More importantly, will he succeed in linking neo-authoritarianism and technological innovation? If he succeeds, China may well become the perfect twenty-first-century dictatorship. As sinologist François Godement of the European Council on Foreign Relations has pointed out, 'Xi's Chinese Dream is a resurrection of Mao's totalitarianism, but with the benefit of technological tools that Mao could only dream of'. 'Communism is the Soviets plus electricity', Lenin once said; a full century later, Xi could well reply, 'Chinese communism is the Party plus artificial intelligence and facial recognition'.

In any case, Xi has the determination, the political instinct, the culture, and the career to achieve his ends. This was the conviction of Eric Li, businessman, political scientist and supporter of the regime, following the Nineteenth Congress. Heedless of the Western media's predictions, which he believes to be erroneous, Li predicted in *The Washington Post* 'that Xi will indeed change China, and the world, for the better', because 'the [P]arty's ability to adapt to changing times by reinventing itself is extraordinary'.

One real threat remains, and I am not the only who sees it: in seeking to turn his country into a leading industrial power by 2049, for the centenary of the People's Republic of China, Xi is unleashing forces that may yet turn on him. A creative and innovating China may not be satisfied with the existing framework, and could in future support calls for political reform. But of how great a magnitude? The fate of the 'new emperor' depends, in part, on the answer.

FURTHER READING & VIEWING

Books (non-fiction)

Becker, Jasper, *Hungry Ghosts: Mao's Secret Famine*, New York: Free Press, 1997.

Billioud, Sébastien and Joël Thoraval, *The Sage and the People: The Confucian Revival in China*, New York: Oxford University Press, 2015.

Brown, Kerry, *CEO, China: The Rise of Xi Jinping*, London: I.B. Tauris, 2016.

Dickson, Bruce J., *The Dictator's Dilemma: The Chinese Communist Party's Strategy for Survival*, New York: Oxford University Press, 2016.

Dikötter, Frank, *The Cultural Revolution: A People's History, 1962–1976*, London: Bloomsbury, 2016.

Elizabeth C. Economy, *The Third Revolution: Xi Jinping and the New Chinese State*, New York: Oxford University Press, 2018.

Fenby, Jonathan, *Will China Dominate the 21st Century?*, Cambridge: Polity, 2014.

Hessler, Peter, *Country Driving: A Journey Through China from Farm to Factory*, New York: Harper, 2010.

Ho, Denise Y., *Curating Revolution: Politics on Display in*

Mao's China, Cambridge: Cambridge University Press, 2017.

Johnson, Ian, *The Souls of China: The Return of Religion After Mao*, New York: Pantheon, 2017.

Lam, Willy Wo-Lap, *Chinese Politics in the Era of Xi Jinping: Renaissance, Reform, or Retrogression?*, London: Routledge, 2015.

Li, Cheng, *Chinese Politics in the Xi Jinping Era: Reassessing Collective Leadership*, Washington, DC: Brookings Institution Press, 2016.

Li Kunwu and Philippe Ôtié, *A Chinese Life* (graphic novel), New York: Harry N. Abrams, 2012.

Lim, Louisa, *The People's Republic of Amnesia, Tiananmen Revisited*, New York: Oxford University Press, 2014.

McGregor, Richard, *The Party: The Secret World of China's Communist Rulers*, New York: Harper Perennial, 2012.

Pei, Minxin, *China's Crony Capitalism: The Dynamics of Regime Decay*, Cambridge, MA: Harvard University Press, 2016.

Osnos, Evan, *Age of Ambition: Chasing Fortune, Truth, and Faith in the New China*, New York: Farrar, Straus and Giroux, 2014.

Ringen, Stein, *The Perfect Dictatorship: China in the 21st Century*, Hong Kong: Hong Kong University Press, 2016.

Rocca, Jean-Louis, *The Making of the Chinese Middle Class: Small Comfort and Great Expectations*, London: Palgrave Macmillan, 2016.

Shambaugh, David, *China's Future*, Cambridge: Polity, 2016.

Short, Philip, *Mao: A Life*, New York: Henry Holt, 2000.

Vogel, Ezra F., *Deng Xiaoping and the Transformation of China*, Cambridge, MA: Belknap Press, 2011.

Xi Jinping: The Governance of China, Vols 1 and 2 (1st edition), Beijing: Foreign Languages Press, 2014.

Yang Jisheng, *Tombstone: The Great Chinese Famine, 1958–1962*, New York: Farrar, Straus and Giroux, 2012.

Zhang Weiwei, *The China Wave: Rise of a Civilizational State*, Hackensack, NJ: World Century Publishing Corporation, 2012.

Books (fiction)

Chan Koonchung, *The Fat Years*, London: Transworld, 2011.

Ma Jian, *The Dark Road: A Novel*, New York: Penguin Books, 2014.

Liu Cixin, *The Three-Body Problem*, New York: Tor Books, 2016.

Liu Zhenyun, *The Cook, the Crook, and the Real Estate Tycoon: A Novel of Contemporary China*, New York: Arcade Publishing, 2015.

Yu Hua, *The Seventh Day: A Novel*, New York: Pantheon, 2015.

Films

Feng Xiaogang, *Youth*, 2017.

Jia Zhangke, *A Touch of Sin*, 2013.

Qu, Vivian, *Angels Wear White*, 2017.

Wang Bing, *Dead Souls*, 2018.

Wu Jing, *Wolf Warrior 2*, 2017.